The Tale of Euphemia and the Goth

ANALECTA GORGIANA

57

General Editor

George Anton Kiraz

Analecta Gorgiana is a collection of long essays and short monographs which are consistently cited by modern scholars but previously difficult to find because of their original appearance in obscure publications. Now conveniently published, these essays are not only vital for our understanding of the history of research and ideas, but are also indispensable tools for the continuation and development of on-going research. Carefully selected by a team of scholars based on their relevance to modern scholarship, these essays can now be fully utilized by scholars and proudly owned by libraries.

The Tale of Euphemia and the Goth

Text and Translation with Notes and Commentary

FRANCIS CRAWFORD BURKITT

GORGIAS PRESS
2007

First Gorgias Press Edition, 2007

Published in the United States of America by Gorgias Press LLC, New Jersey

This edition is a facsimile reprint of the original edition published as parts of *Euphemia and the Goth* by Williams & Norgate, London, 1913

ISBN 978-1-59333-876-3

ISSN 1935-6854

GORGIAS PRESS
46 Orris Ave., Piscataway, NJ 08854 USA
www.gorgiaspress.com

The paper used in this publication meets the minimum requirements of the American National Standards.

Printed in the United States of America

A NOTE FROM THE PRESS EDITOR

This volume is composed of sections from F. C. Burkitt's larger work *Euphemia and the Goth*, now available from Gorgias Press under the title *The Acts of the Edessan Martyrs Shmona, Guria and Habib, and their Deliverance of Euphemia.* As only the tale of Euphemia and the Goth are included in the present volume, some sections have been edited so as to remove any confusing internal references to the tales of the Edessan Martyrs Shmona, Guria and Habib. The Table of Contents and the Lists of Illustrations are new and refer to the [bracketed], Gorgias edition page numbers, and the index has been carefully edited, but still refers to the original page numbers. Nothing of the author's has been changed, only consolidated in order to make this volume coherent.

TABLE OF CONTENTS

List of Illustrations

ERRATA.

p. 53, l. 10 *for* promites *read* promises
p. 73, l. 15 „ thans „ thanks
p. 73, l. 28 „ *chaneed* „ chanced

---

p. ܣܛ 24 *for* ܦ̈ܣܝܢܬܐ *read* ܦ̈ܣܝܢܬܐ
p. ܣܒ 10 *for* *see* p. *read* *see* p. 72
p. ܣܘ 15 *for* 1 *read* 2
p. ܪܟ 17 *for* ܪܐܬܟܬܒ *read* ܕܐܬܟܬܒ
p. ܟܛ 8 *for* ܕܒܝܢܬ *read* ܕܒܝܢܬ

VIEW FROM NEAR THE WEST GATE OF EDESSA.

1. *S. Theodore (reputed tomb of Ephraim Syrus).* 2. *Modern private house.*
3. *Direction of Beth Alah Ḳiḳla.*

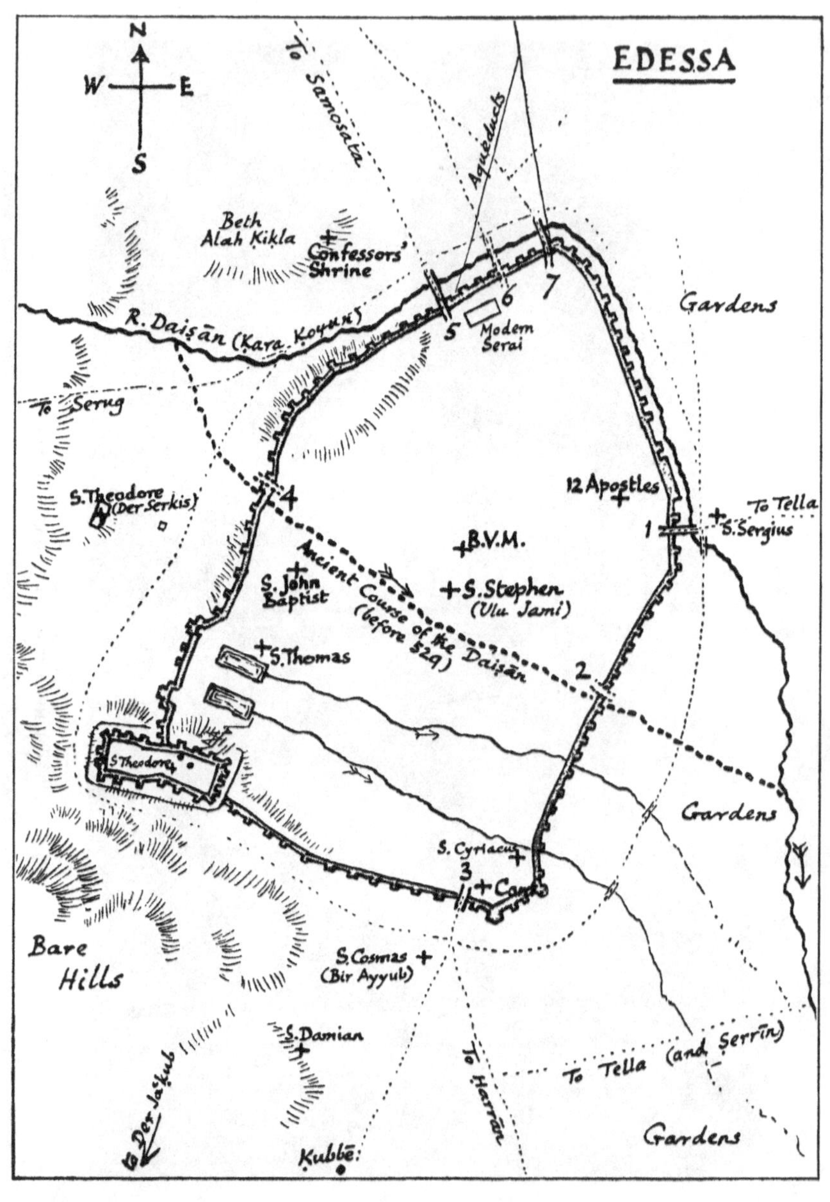
EDESSA
N
W
E
S
To Samosata
Aqueducts
Beth
Alah Ḳiḳla
Confessors' Shrine
R. Daiṣān (Ḳara Ḳoyun)
5
6
7
Modern Serai
Gardens
To Serug
S. Theodore (Der Serkis)
4
12 Apostles
To Tella
1
S. Sergius
B.V.M.
Ancient Course of the Daiṣān (before 529)
S. John Baptist
S. Stephen (Ulu Jami)
S. Thomas
2
S. Theodore
Gardens
S. Cyriacus
3
Bare Hills
S. Cosmas (Bir Ayyub)
S. Damian
To Der Ja'ḳub
To Ḥarrān
To Tella (and Serrin)
Gardens
Kubbē

Gates of Edessa—Urfa:

1. Bey's Gate *(Bek Kapusi)* = Great Gate [Josh. Styl.].
2. Theatre Gate [Josh. Styl.].
3. Harran Gate = Sundial Gate [Bar Hebr.]; G. of Beth Shemesh [Chron.].
4. W. Gate *(Bāb Essākib, Daghlar Kapu)* = G. of the "Arches" [Josh.; Ḥabbib].
5. Samosata Gate = old N. Gate.
6. Serai Gate.
7. New Gate *(Yeni Kapu)*.

The Cross close to N°. 3, marked Conf., is the New Church and Monastery of the Confessors, mentioned by Bar Hebraeus and in Rahmani's Chronicle. The large Bastion just south of it is probably what was called *Rāmath Dauḳē* (i.e. Watchmen's Height). Near the Church of S. Theodore in the Citadel is marked the position of the two great Columns. S. Theodore outside the walls, now the Armenian Monastery of S. Sergius *(Der Serkis)*, is the building shewn in the Frontispiece. The modern Armenian Cathedral must be very nearly on the site of S. John Baptist.

ABOUT EUPHEMIA AND THE GOTH.

§ 1.

From the time that I first read the story of Euphemia in the Nitrian MS. I had no doubt that it was of Syriac origin. The Greek version had been known to me chiefly from a fragmentary MS. at Emmanuel College, Cambridge, but it seemed altogether inferior and secondary compared with the Syriac. As however Professor von Dobschütz, in his admirable edition of the Greek text of the tale, maintains that it, and not the Syriac, is the original, it is necessary to indicate the reasons which incline me to the contrary opinion.

A tale about the local Saints of Edessa might naturally be supposed to have originated there, and any other hypothesis needs either express external testimony or strong internal arguments. It will be convenient to begin by enumerating Prof. v. Dobschütz's arguments, to be found on p. L of his edition.

"1. Not only is no Syriac text of *Euphemia* known, but also there is no reference to the tale in Jacob of Serug's Homilies or in the rest of Syriac literature".

The production of two Syriac MSS., one of them as old as the 9th century, is not perhaps a complete answer to this, though it goes a considerable way. It may be further urged, with reference to the silence of Jacob of Serug and others, that the same argument might be used to prove that the "Hymn of the Soul" in the Acts of Thomas was not a Syriac original. For Jacob composed a Homily on the Palace which S. Thomas built, but he is silent about the great Hymn; and, on the other hand, the Hymn is both extant in Greek and is also the subject of an Encomium by Niceta of Thessalonica! The fact is, that we do not possess an approximately complete or representative *Corpus* of Syriac Literature, in the same way that we possess it for the Byzantine Greek and Mediaeval Latin Literatures. What we have is the contents of a single monastic Library, supplemented by late collections from elsewhere. And the special interest of the story of Euphemia is its secular tone; it is only in some of the secondary Greek texts that the heroine becomes a nun.

"2. All the Greek texts go back to a single literary work, which shews no trace of being a translation from the Syriac".

Now that the Syriac is before us we see that the "translation" was so free that linguistic traces of a foreign style are scarcely to be looked for. The Syriac is as much fresher, less ecclesiastical, more like a folk-tale, than v. Dobschütz's text, as that text is than those in the *Menaea*.

"3. The quotations from the Bible are taken from the Septuagint".

In the Syriac the few Biblical passages that occur (mostly from the Psalms) are given in according with the Peshitta. The translator, whether Greek or Syrian, simply made use of the familiar words of his own Bible.

"4. The mother and daughter, Sophia and Euphemia, have Greek names".

But these names are hardly more foreign on Mesopotamian ground than "Sophia" and "Euphemia" are in England. Euphemia was the name of a famous martyr, actually mentioned in the Edessene Chronicle (§ 83) [1]).

"5. The character of the Tale itself is that of the Greek Novel".

Our knowledge of the range of Syriac Literature is less than that of Greek Literature. Yet Syriac Literature includes Romances such as the Acts of Thomas, with its brilliant sketches of the minor characters. The dull "Romance of Julian" is a regular historical novel. But indeed the East has always been famous for the telling of Tales: the Story of Euphemia is at least as near to the Arabian Nights as it is to the tale of Clytemnestra and Cassandra.

It is, I venture to think, obvious that no safe conclusion can be reached from these general considerations. The nature and *provenance* of the Syriac MSS are equally indecisive. The 9th century Nitrian MS was written by one Simeon, who copied it for his own use (Wright, *CBM* 1110): the contents of the volume are miscellaneous, same of the stories being taken from such well-known sources as the Historia Lausiaca, no doubt at second or third hand. Most of the twenty-six items are found elsewhere in Syriac MSS, and one of them, the History of Simeon of Kephar ᶜAbdin, is certainly of Syriac origin [2]). The Paris MS was written in the

1) Curiously enough, here also is a mention of a miracle wrought in connexion with a Coffin *(gluskmā)*.

2) See also Appendix I for another Syriac tale from the same MS.

13th century at Antioch, and it also is a collection of edifying tales. At the end of *Euphemia* we find a Note, as follows:

"Here endeth the story of the miracle that the Holy Confessors performed on Euphemia who was betrothed to the Goth in Edessa: it was copied from an old book that was written in the royal city of Constantinople by John the Monk and Recluse".

So far as it goes, this certainly would suggest a Greek origin for the tale, but the Note is not confirmed by the Nitrian MS, written some three or four centuries earlier. And even if it be regarded as a serious piece of information, it does not legitimate the existing Greek text, as edited by v. Dobschütz, against the Syriac text here published [1]).

Thus everything goes back to the internal evidence of the two texts themselves. And here I feel the verdict is clear and unhesitating. The Syriac text is in every way more original and superior to the Greek. It is difficult indeed to offer any formal demonstration, for neither text is a literal rendering of the other. But to give an idea of the characteristics of the two texts I will set down a few quite literal English translations of parallel passages side by side.

1. (The actual beginning of the tale).

Syriac.	*Greek.*
§ 4 =	*v. Dobschütz*, p. 150.
In the year 707 by the	In the year 707 of Alex-

1) The phrase "royal city" *(Medīnath Malkūtha)* makes the conjecture possible that this part of the colophon originally belonged not to *Euphemia*, but to the Story of the Wife of Patricius and the Merchant of Harran (Appendix I).

reckoning of the Greeks the [Huns] [1] had come forth [into the Roman territories], and they captured many captives and laid waste the country and came as far as Edessa.	ander King of Macedon that evil and destructive nation the Huns, having come into the Roman territories and laid waste various places and taken many captives, arrived as far as the district round Edessa.
And Addai the Stratelates of those days did not give permission for the *Foederati* to go out against them, because of treachery in the midst,	[*no equivalent*].
and for this cause the armies of the Romans came down and lived in Edessa some time.	For this cause armed forces gathered from various regions occupied the city and lived in it a long time.
Now a certain Goth....	Now a certain Goth....

[The point to notice is that the clause which gives definite local and political information is absent from the Greek].

2. (Sophia's ejaculation, when against her better judgement she consents to let the Goth marry Euphemia).

§ 10 =	*v. Dobschütz*, p. 156_7.
"God of the orphans and the widows, come to my help! My God, this business	"Thou, Lord, Father of the orphans and Judge of the widows, look upon what

1) The Nitrian MS has 'Persians' on an erasure. The Huns are mentioned below in § 35, along with the Persians, as in the Greek. On the Syriac text of the first sentence see the Note on the passage.

is entrusted to thee, to whom alone it is revealed!"

is being done, and do not look away from my orphan child or helpless me! For trusting in thy good Providence I am enduring the marriage of my unhappy daughter with an unknown man, who calls thee to be witness and surety of his own promites".

[On p. LIV Prof. v. Dobschütz says: "Besondere Freude aber hat der Verfasser offenbar an der Komposition von Gebeten .... hier führt ein griechischer Theologe die Feder". Now that we have the Syriac original, we can see exactly how much is due to the Greek theologian!]

3. (Sophia visits the shrine of the Confessors with Euphemia and the Goth before they go away to his home).

§ 13 =

And when they had sealed their prayer with a tear, the mother of the girl drew near and took hold of her by her right hand and set her upon the Coffin [1]) of the Confessors, saying to her false

v. Dobschütz, p. 158_{14}.

And as they were standing by the reliquary of the Holy ones she said to that wicked man:

"Not otherwise will I entrust my daughter to thee, except first having

1) The Syriac has *Gluskmā*, an adaptation of γλωσσόκομον (Joh. XIII 29), as in *S. & G.* 67, and also in Barhebraeus, *Chr. Syr.* 327_{12}. The Greek has λάρναξ and σορόσ.

son-in-law: "Give me for a surety the hidden Power that dwells on these Holy ones! Both thou dost know, and they do, according as thou dost treat her!"

touched the bier of the Holy ones thou acknowledge them as sureties that thou wilt do nothing to cause the girl pain, but will treat her will all due respect and harmony".

[The Syriac uses the technical term in use at the Shrine; the Greek uses synonyms. For Sophia to put the girl on the Coffin, as in the Syriac, may have seemed wanting in respect; the Greek implies a mere conventional touching. And, finally, I venture to claim (all due allowance being made for difference of national idiom, and for the execrable taste of later Greek prose generally), that the Syriac is literature, and that the Greek is not. This is equally the case whether we take the Syriac from the Nitrian MS (here given), or from the slightly curtailed text of the Paris MS].

4. (Euphemia, now degraded to be a slave-girl, has a son: the Goth's wife is jealous of her).

§ 20 =

And when the days had come near for the girl to bear, there was born to her a man-child, and he was like his father exceedingly; and when the wife of the Goth saw the baby that he was like her husband she was struck with envy, and with

v. Dobschütz, p. 168_6.

And when the days were accomplished the girl bove a man-child, in looks exactly like the Goth. And when the woman saw it she was taken with such fury as in every way to confirm in herself the opinion that she must anyhow kill the child.

great indignation she said to her husband: "Look and see how like he is to thee! Now therefore cavilling and lying are of no use to thee!" And when many times with indignation she had said this to him, he saith to her: "Thou hast authority over her; every thing thou dost wish to do to her, do, for she is thy slave".

But to her husband she said: "It is vain for thee to contend that thou hast not had intercourse with the girl, for the child that has been born quite refutes that, he being so exceedingly like to thee". But he again kept asserting the contrary, saying this indeed is not true, but (it is true) that thou hast authority to use the girl as thou wilt, as she is thy slave and subject to everything that seems good to thee".

[I cannot believe that the vigour of the Syriac here can be due to a translator: the gruff answer of the Goth to his nagging spouse is ever so much more effective than the unnecessary lie in the Greek. And note the exaggeration in the first sentence: *χαρακτῆρα φέρων ἀπαραλλάκτωσ προσεοικότα τῷ Γότθῳ* is an absurd phrase to use of a baby a few months old. The Syriac really implies no more than that the child of the Syrian girl had blue eyes, and perhaps a promise of light hair].

5. (Sophia, to make the Goth perjure himself, pretends to be anxious to have news of Euphemia).

§ 37 =	*v. Dobschütz*, p. 188_{14}.
Sophia his mother-in-law began to ask him, saying:	Sophia .... asks him, saying:

"What is thy tale, my son? And what is the tale of Euphemia my daughter? How did the journey treat you? Has a son been born to you? Is it a boy or a girl? For I have been much in anxiety about you, because of the length of the journey".

"How by God's help did you bear the journey? And how did my daughter recover from the journey, she being with child? For I was in much anxiety about you, lest some misfortune should meet you on the way, but I was especially grieved about Euphemia my daughter, because she was with child".

[On p. LIV attention is drawn by v. Dobschütz to Sophia's speech as a notable example of the narrator making his characters talk piously. I cannot believe that a translator would have left the piety out. The last sentence is much longer and perhaps more original in the Paris MS: "For I have been in much anxiety about you, on account of having let my daughter go over, and how you went forth hence. And for this I was anxious, because a long journey ye had to go, that it should not have happened to my daughter from the fatigue of the journey"].

These extracts are probably enough; they could indeed be multiplied indefinitely, but what I have quoted gives the reader a fair idea of the characteristics of the two texts. In every way the Syriac is more natural, more secular, more unconventional. In a word, it is more original, and in what follows I shall venture to treat it as such [1]).

1) The relative excellence of the two Syriac MSS in details is discussed in the next chapter.

§ 2.

What are we to make of the tale of Euphemia? With what kind of commendatory letters are we to hand it over to the historians and to the students of Comparative Religion? "Good wine needs no bush", and it might be thought that such an excellent tale is better without any Introduction. There are however one or two points which it seems proper to bring forward here, as some of them might easily escape notice.

The story itself is laid in the year 396 A.D. and the years immediately following. But the narrator has only learned it from the old Verger, the *Paramonarius*, who tells it in order that it may not be unknown to succeeding generations. This brings us down another 30 years at least, so that the earliest date we could possibly assign to it is 430 A.D., with every probability that it is later still. We therefore see at once that it forms no part of the great series of which the Doctrine of Addai, the Acts of Sharbel and the Acts of Guria and Shmona and of Ḥabbib form links. When the tale was first being written down, the Shrine of the Confessors built by Bishop Abraham in 350 was about a century old and the cult of the Saints themselves thoroughly well established in Edessa. Whether we treat the story of Euphemia as history or myth, it can neither endanger the historicity of Shmona, Guria and Ḥabbib, nor on the other hand legitimate the details of their legend, which had already received its final shape when the episode of the Goth is alleged to have taken place.

It should further be noticed that the names and dates mentioned in the story exhibit a considerable,

8

though not quite accurate, knowledge of Edessene affairs. The invasions of the Huns really did take place in 395—6 [1]). Moreover the General (*Stratelates*) in command at the time was really named Addai. "Joshua Stylites", writing at Edessa in 507, speaks of the devastation then wrought, when all Syria was delivered into the hand of these same Huns "through the treachery of the Prefect Rufinus and by the supineness of Addai the General" [2]). The name of Eulogius for a Bishop of Edessa is also appropriate, though Eulogius was Bishop from 379 to 387, the Bishops of Edessa during the time of our tale being Cyrus (died 396), Silvanus (died 398), and Peḳīda. It is one of the notable peculiarities of the story of Euphemia that the author is better informed about the secular history of Edessa than about ecclesiastical affairs.

I do not think we need to look for theological considerations to explain how a Goth comes to be the villain of an Edessene legend. Professor v. Dobschütz (p. LV) suggests that Edessa was famed for its orthodoxy and the Goths were known to be Arians, and that this is why the Goth is painted in such dark colours. But the Goth's orthodoxy or heterodoxy is never mentioned,

---

1) The Edessene Chronicle specifies July 395, and within a year Cyrillona tells us that a fresh incursion was threatened.

2) ܒܝܕ ܢܟܝܠܘܬܐ ܕܪܘܦܝܢܘܣ ܗܘܦܪܟܐ ܘܒܦܫܝܪܘܬܐ ܕܐܕܝ ܣܛܪܛܠܛܝܣ (*J St* § 9). On the treachery of Rufinus, see *Gibbon* III 224. It is convenient to go on calling the author of the Chronicle edited by Wright "Joshua the Stylite", though there is good reason for doubting that this was the name of the author. What is not doubted is that the author was an eyewitness of what he describes, and that he wrote at Edessa in 507 A.D.

and the good people of Edessa had quite sufficient reasons of their own for misliking the Teutonic mercenaries of the Byzantine Emperor. Let us listen once more to "Joshua the Stylite":

"Those who came to our aid", says he (§ LXXXVI), "plundered us almost as much as our enemies.... Because the courts and inns of the city of Edessa were not sufficient for them, they lodged with the artisans in their shops. Before the eyes of every one they illused the women in the streets and houses. From old women, widows and poor, they took oil, wood, salt, and other things, for their own expenses; and they kept them from their own work to wait upon them. In short, they harassed every one, both great and small, and there was not a person left who did not suffer some harm from them".

And again, in April, 506, "because the city of Edessa was not sufficient for the Goths, they were quartered also in the villages, and likewise in all the convents, large and small, that were around the city. Not even those who lived in solitude were allowed to dwell in the quiet which they loved, because upon them too they were quartered in their convents.

"Because they did not live at their own expense from the very first day they came, they became so gluttonous in their eating and drinking, that some of them who had regaled themselves on the tops of the houses went forth by night, quite stupefied with too much wine, and stepped out into empty space and fell headlong down, and so departed this life by an evil end. Others as they were sitting and drinking sank into slumber, and fell from the housetops and died on the spot. Others again suffered agonies on their beds from eating too much. Some poured boiling water into the ears of those who waited upon them for trifling faults. Others went into a garden to take vegetables, and when the gardener arose to prevent them they slew him with an arrow, and his blood was not avenged. Others still, as their wickedness increased and there was no one to check them, since those on whom they were quartered behaved with great discretion and did every thing exactly as they wished, because they gave them no opportunity for doing them harm, were overcome by their own rage and slew one another. That there were among them others who lived decently", continues our Chronicler, addressing his patron, Abbot Sergius, "is not concealed from thy knowledge, for it is impossible that in a large army like this there should not be some such persons found" (§ XCVI).

It was not the agreement of the Goths with the Heresiarch of Alexandria that so unfavourably impressed the people of Edessa, but rather their unmistakeable likeness to their cousin Mr Thomas Atkins. As we read the description in "Joshua" it needs but little effort to imagine that we are listening to the complaint of a Bengali Babu about some European soldiers who have got out of hand. The European often appears rude, ungovernable and intemperate to the native of Asia, and if the tale of Euphemia really originated in Edessa or in the neighbourhood it is not surprising that the Goth is represented in a very unfavourable light. It is not necessary to assume that the story is later than 506, for the householders of Edessa may very well have had earlier experiences of Gothic soldiers billeted upon them, especially in 396 and the following years.

§ 3.

It is fashionable now-a-days to regard large numbers of the Kalendar Saints as minor deities of the pagan world, and to treat the Legends told about them not as so much untrustworthy or perverted historical reminiscence, but rather as pagan myth in a more or less Christian disguise. That this is true in certain cases is demonstrated practically beyond a doubt [1]). In such legends it is unscientific to rationalise. But the case is different here: at any rate the matter is not quite simple.

There are, it is true, certain features in the Story of Euphemia which do suggest that the Confessors stand in the place that Dr Rendel Harris has vindicated for the Heavenly Twins. According to Dr Harris the Twins are the patrons of the bride-chamber and bestow benedictions on the newly-married [2]), and are also the avengers of perjury [3]). This is exactly the rôle that the Confessors play in our tale. If then we knew nothing more of Shmona, Guria and Ḥabbib than our tale tells us, we might be inclined to regard them as mere surrogates for the Great Twin Brethren. It is true that neither the names nor the dates fit, but that is a trifle! In this case, however, we are dealing with Saints who are really historical, to whatever extent their Legend may have received unhistorical touches. It is therefore not necessary here to suppose that the earliest and purest texts

1) The best instance perhaps is SS. Florus and Laurus, with which Dr Rendel Harris's book on *The Dioscuri in the Christian Legends* starts off.

2) *Harris*, p. 15. 3) *Harris*, p. 56.

of our tale will exhibit "Dioscurism" in the clearest form. As a matter of fact, the most "Dioscuric" trait of all is only found in the late and rhetorical Greek Encomium of Arethas, in which he makes the Confessors carry away Euphemia on white steeds (*λευκοῖσ γοῦν ἔποχοι ἵπποισ*, *v. Dobschütz*, p. 221_8)[1]. So far as the earlier forms are concerned this method of transit is only suggested by the lively imagination of Sophia: "Guria, Shmona and Ḥabbib", she says to the Goth (§ 40 = p. 150_4), "they became swift steeds for Euphemia, and delivered her from your hands!" The word used (*rkūba*) is quite vague, and signifies "carriage" as well as "animal ridden": in fact, the Greek has *ὀξύτατον ὄχημα* (*v. Dobschütz*, 192_5). This point about the steeds is a mere detail, but it is worth notice as warning us that detached mythological features in the Legend of a Saint do not always belong to the original form of the story.

I should like to point out that another way of treating this Legend of Euphemia is open to us, a frankly rationalistic way. We are dealing with a story that seems to have originated on the spot with which it deals, a story which dealt not with the remote past, but with real places and contemporary conditions of life. How do such stories begin? What is there to prevent us taking the tale of Euphemia for plain fact?

What stands in the way, of course, is the Miracle. Opinions differ about the theoretical possibility of "Mi-

---

1) It has not escaped Prof. v. Dobschütz that this may be described as a *Dioskurenzug*. He remarks very sensibly (p. XLII): "Man sieht, wie leicht solche Motive sich einschleichen: das Thauma lässt in der Tat die Art der Entrückung ganz unberührt; hier klaffte eine Lücke; die Phantasie war nicht müssig, sie auszufüllen!"

racles", but I suppose no one at the present day will seriously accept the story of Euphemia's transit in one night from the land of the Goths to the Shrine of the Confessors as either probable or credible. Yet the story is in some respects so unlike the usual type of hagiological tale, that I find it difficult to believe that a real occurence does not lie at the back of it. As a matter of evidence we have to distinguish three witnesses. First comes the Narrator: let us suppose that he really did hear this tale from the Paramonarius. To the Narrator, then, we will put down the literary form, and a good deal of the speeches, regarded as literary compositions. Then comes the Paramonarius, an old man, who had no doubt often told the tale to pious folk, and we may imagine it lost nothing in his hands, especially so far as concerned the part played by his patrons the Confessors. Then we come to the real witness, to Euphemia, whose tale, poor girl, we have not got, but only the tale which the old Paramonarius tells for her.

There are one or two features in the tale as we have it, which seem to me curious. The first is, that in all the last part Euphemia is silent. Her mother Sophia acts for her and speaks for her. She says not one word to the Goth, good or bad, and she makes no answer to the Stratelates. It looks to me as if she had mentally broken down.

Another point in the tale that is left unexplained, and therefore may lead us to a clue, is the mention in § 24 (= p. 141_1) of "the people of the city" where the Goths were. The Goths, after the death of Euphemia's mistress, the Goth's wife, drag Euphemia to the tomb and shut her up there. "And while they were dragging her along and beating her the people of the city saw her, and they were grieved for her". And then the Goths "take thought lest the people of the city should come and let her out, and accordingly roll a big stone against the door to keep her safe prisoner all night [1]). But what the Goths could roll by day the "people of the city" could roll away by night. It is evident from this passage, the important parts of which have no equivalent in the Greek, that these Goths are to be thought of as settled in some place within the Roman Empire, somewhere in Anatolia or even nearer to Edessa, where the Roman Law was normally administered, although in this particular case the "judge" lives some way off. And further, it is evident that the native provincials had no particular love for the fair-haired barbarians, quartered in their midst in accordance with the exigences of Imperial policy. Is it not possible that "the people of the city" did take Euphemia out of the tomb by night, while the Goths were occupied (as usual) in drinking?

Suppose this were the case — and it is not such a very improbable supposition — I imagine that the rescuers would find Euphemia in a state of collapse. The townsfolk, among whom we know that she used to go to market, knew that she came from Edessa. They would naturally want to get her out of the way as soon as possible, and some one who is going towards Mesopotamia takes her. She was probably quite out of her mind from the shock, a condition which would secure her respectful treatment in the Orient. Most likely she

---

1) According to the Paris MS the "people of the city" did actually plan this, but the text of the Nitrian MS is preferable.

was speechless or incoherent, and little could be got out of her beyond "Urhai! Confessors of Urhai!" It is not necessary to suppose that she travelled with the same company all the way. At last Euphemia finds herself outside the walls of Edessa, by the knoll on which stands the Shrine of the Confessors. It would be the first considerable group of buildings that she would come to on her way from the West. She is quite unable to explain how she got there: the last that she can recollect is the horrible tomb, and the rotting body of the Gothic woman whom she herself had killed. But she recognises the Confessors' Shrine and she goes inside — and interrupts the service. Even as the story is told by the Paramonarius, whose chief concern no doubt is the honour and glory of the Saints over whose Reliquary he watches, we can see that Euphemia's story was quite incoherent. She was so changed, that at first Sophia did not recognise her daughter. She had reached home indeed, but she was little more than a wreck.

All this of course is frankly imaginative reconstruction of the transmitted story, based on hints which are let drop here and there. But it seems to me easier to believe that something of this kind happened, than to suppose that the story is altogether a work of fiction from beginning to end. It is difficult to regard Shmona, Guria, and Ḥabbib as being really Dioscuri in a Christian dress; rather they may be regarded as having stepped into the place which the Dioscuri certainly filled in some other lands, and may once have filled in Edessa, as the Guardians of good faith.

§ 4.

And what was their own fate? What happened to the Coffin from off which the Goth received Euphemia? We pass down seven hundred years, to 1144 A.D. After some vicissitudes Edessa is in Christian hands again, under Joscelin the Second, grandson of the Lord of Courtenay. But when on Tuesday the 28th of November, 1144, Zengi the Atabek appeared before the walls of Edessa with his Turks, Joscelin and his men-at-arms were far away, somewhere near Antioch, and the town had to defend itself as well as it could. The Turks were encamped "over against the Sundial Gate by the Church of the Confessors", that is to say they were south of the town, near the SE. angle of the town-wall, which was where the Sundial Gate, now called the Ḥarran Gate, was situated. Close by, inside the town, was the New Church of the Confessors, distinct from the ancient Shrine outside the walls on the NW. of Edessa. But just as in 503, the precious Relics had been brought inside the town during the war. For the rest we will leave Bar Hebraeus to tell the story. "They pitched their camp over against the Gate of the Sundial, by the Church of the Confessors, and raised against it seven mangonels [1]) with bowmen shooting arrows like showers of rain. And the citizens all of them, both great and small, and even the monks from the Mountain, were standing on the wall and fighting; and all the women

---

1) My readers may remember Richard of Cornwall, who "makede him a Castel of a milne-post" at the Battle of Lewis: the ballad suggests that "he weened that the wheels were *mangonels*".

were handing out stones and water and food to the fighters. And when those outside mined underground and came up to the wall, those inside countermined and made a sortie, and killed those whom they found in the mine, and then returned and built up the wall where the mine was" [1]). This, by the way, is the siege of Edessa of which Gibbon says (VI 447) that the city was "feebly defended by a timorous and disloyal crowd of Orientals"! [2])

The Turks continued to mine the walls, especially two of the towers, "and when the towers were near to fall, Zengi the Atabek sent to the Edessenes, and said 'Take two men from us as hostages, and send two men to us that they may see how near the towers are to fall, and surrender the city before ye be taken prisoners at the sword's point and perish!'" But Papias, the captain of the Franks in Edessa, trusted that Joscelin would come to relieve him in time, and so he refused to capitulate. "Then the Turks set fire to the wooden supports by which the towers were propped up, and they fell; and when the Turks began to enter by the breach, the citizens from within with Papias and the Bishop [3]) stood in the breach and kept the Turks from entering, and the breach was filled with heaps of the slain both of besieged and besiegers. But when all the people were congregated at the breach, the Turks saw that the wall was deserted of fighting men, and they set ladders and got up; and when those inside saw that the Turks had

1) Bar-Hebraeus, *Chronicon* 326.

2) Gibbon was probably following William of Tyre XVI 4, 5, who regarded the people of Edessa as 'a nation of shopkeepers'.

3) Read ܐܦܣܩܘܦܐ (without ••): evidently Bishop Basil is meant.

got possession of the wall they lost heart and began to flee to the citadel.

"And from that moment", continues Bar-Hebraeus, or rather the excellent source which he is transcribing, "what mouth does not hesitate to tell, what finger does not tremble to write, about the consternation that reigned at 9 o'clock that Saturday morning, the 13th January![1]) The Turks entered with drawn sword and it drank the blood of old and young, of men and women, of priests and deacons, of monks and anchorites, of nuns and virgins, of children, of bridegrooms, of brides. Alas, for the bitter tale! The City of Abgar, the Friend of Christ, was trodden down in the dust for our sins! Oh, the misery of it! Parents deserted their children and children their parents, the mother forgot her love for her little ones, and every one ran away up the hill!

"But the aged priests who were carrying the Coffins of the Confessors, when they saw the wrath, of which the Prophet said 'The Wrath of the Lord I will endure because I have sinned', for that very reason did not flee themselves, nor did they cease from prayer until the sword silenced them. And afterwards they were found with their vestments stained with their blood.

"Many of the mothers gathered their children as a hen does its brood, and waited, that either they might die together by the sword or might be taken to slavery in a body"[2]).

Bar-Hebraeus goes on to tell us that the gates of the citadel were shut against the fugitives, till at last the

1) The text has "3rd", but it must be wrong: read ܝܓ for ܓ.
2) *Chronicle* 327.

garrison recognised the face of Papias among them. Meanwhile thousands had been crushed to death, or were slain by the Turkish arrows. At last the Atabek gave orders for the slaughter to cease, and then Bishop Basil was found as he was being dragged along naked and barefoot, one of a string of captives, by the Turks. "And when Zengi the Atabeg saw him, he was struck by the nobility of his face and asked who he was. And when he learned that it was the Metropolitan, he gave orders to find a dress for him and had him brought into his tent. And he began blaming him, because they had not surrendered the city and so saved the wretched population from slaughter. But the Bishop replied: 'It has pleased Divine Providence to give to thee victory such as this and great and splendid renown among the kings, thy brothers; and to us unfortunates it has been given to look our liege lord in the face, in that we were no traitors and did not break our oaths!' And his words pleased the Atabeg, and he said to him: 'The truth hast thou spoken, Oh Mitrān! For to God and to men dear are they that keep their oaths, and above all those who persevere unto death!"

With this tragic tale the Coffin of the Confessors disappears from history. Neither the Dioscuri of the ancient world nor the venerated remains of the Christian martyrs availed to stay the inundation of Islam. But it was a gallant end. The spirit of the cult to which Euphemia appealed survived in Bishop Basil, and the homage which the Atabek paid to good faith, the champions of which Shmona, Guria and Ḥabbib had come to be in the eyes of their fellow-citizens, has proved a more enduring tribute than a costly mediaeval shrine.

ON THE TEXT OF THE WORK HERE EDITED.

For the story of Euphemia we have two MSS, the Nitrian MS in London (L) and the MS from Antioch in Paris (P).

L. — British Museum, Add. 14649, "written in a good regular hand of the 9th century" (*Wright*) by Simeon, a monk, who copied it for his own use. One Simeon, a priest of Tagrit (on the Tigris, S. of Mosul), gave it to the Nitrian Library: it does not appear whether this person was, or was not, identical with Simeon who wrote the book. L contains 26 pious tales, some of which are well known and taken from Greek sources. *Euphemia* is N°. 17: N°. 18 is the Story of the Merchant from Ḥarran at Constantinople, printed in the Appendix to this volume: N°. 20 is the Story of Simeon of Kephar ʿAbdin, which is surely a Syriac original. [Wright, *CBM*, pp. 1108—1111].

P. — Bibliothèque Nationale, *Ms. Orient.* 234, written at Antioch in the 13th century, is also a collection of pious tales, of which *Euphemia* is N°. 38. It contains several of the pieces found in L, but not in the same order. In the 13th century P appears to have been at Serin-Castra in Tur ʿAbdin. [Zotenberg, *Cat. des Mss. Fonds syriaque*, pp. 182—185].

Besides L and P we have the Greek edited by v. Dobschütz, in which he distinguishes two types $\mathfrak{G}^{A}$ and $\mathfrak{G}^{B}$.

L and P differ considerably in minor points, just as $\mathfrak{G}^{A}$ and $\mathfrak{G}^{B}$ do, but their differences do not correspond at all to anything in the Greek [1]). Indeed the Greek and the Syriac differ so much in character (as noticed in the general section about *Euphemia*) that we may almost always accept the combinations L $\mathfrak{G}$ against P, and P $\mathfrak{G}$ against L, as giving the original reading. Similarly, it may be added, the agreement of $\mathfrak{G}^{A}$ or $\mathfrak{G}^{B}$ with the Syriac should be regarded as giving the original reading of the Greek translation.

To take this latter point first, v. Dobschütz is right in § 24 to read δίκην λεόντων (= $\mathfrak{G}^{A}$) and not δίκην λέγοντεσ (= $\mathfrak{G}^{B}$), for both L and P have "like lions". Again in § 24, καὶ τῆσ τοῦ σώματοσ δυσωδίασ ἀρκούσησ πρὸσ ἀναίρεσιν τῆσ κόρησ (= $\mathfrak{G}^{A}$) is better than τὴν τοῦ σώματοσ δυσωδίαν μὴ φέρουσα ἡ κόρη (= $\mathfrak{G}^{B}$), because L and P have "the stink of that corpse grew more stifling *and was killing her*". On the other hand the Syriac MSS support παραμονάριοσ for the Custodian's title against the προσμονάριοσ accepted by v. Dobschütz: in general, however, it may be said that $\mathfrak{G}^{B}$ is appreciably further away from the Syriac than $\mathfrak{G}^{A}$, and the publication of the Syriac evidence will call for very little change in v. Dobschütz's Greek text.

To decide between L and P is a more difficult matter. The fact that L is about 300 years older than P is perhaps balanced by the claim of P to have been copied

1) It should be added that $\mathfrak{G}^{B}$ in *Euphemia* in no way corresponds to $\mathfrak{G}^{2}$ in *Shmona and Guria*.

from an old book. Moreover the monk Simeon, who wrote L for his own use, may be supposed to have been free to make whatever alterations in this non-canonical tale that may have seemed good to him. On examination, we find the following features:

1. *Orthography*. In matters of orthography P is sensibly inferior to L. Characteristic of P are forms like ܠܐܒܐ, ܣܐܡܐ (poison), ܟܒܝܠ, ܐܘܦܝܡܝܐ (for ܐܘܦܡܝܐ), ܐܣܛܪܐܛܠܐܛܝܣ. [1]) The extra ܝ after the 3rd. sing. fem. perf., which is frequent in L, rarely appears, yet ܐܬ̣ܬ݂ܝ occurs both in L and in P (57_1). We may notice ܣܝܐܘܘܗ̇ P 59_3 65_7, ܫ̈ܝܐܕܡ P 67_9, ܡܣܐܟܘܢ P 60_7, where L has the shorter forms ܣܝܐܘܗ̇, ܫ̈ܝܕܡ, ܡܣܟܘܢ. At 51_5 59_{12} ܡܩܘܢ and ܢܣܩܘܢ occur in P. For the 3rd. pl. perf. fem. we find in 65_1 ܒ̈ܬ݂ܕܡ L, but ܬܒܘ P (a blunder); in 65_3 ܢ̈ܩܦ݂ܡ L, but ܢ̈ܩܦ݂ܝ P; in 67_{10} both L and P have ܩ̈ܪܡ [2]). Besides these, L in 50_{14} has ܫ̈ܬ݂ܕܡ.

The rare form ܚܕܝܐ ('rejoiced') occurs in L, p. 62_4, where P has ܚܕܝ.

The word ܕܝܚܣܩܘܠܡܘܢ ('affidavit') is correctly written only in L. In P it is written ܕܝܣܩܘܐܠܝܘܢ (e.g. 70_{16}) [3]).

1) At 62_{18} the absolute state of ܫܒܝܬܐ (a captive girl) is ܫ݂ܒܝ in L, but ܫ݂ܐܒܝ in P.

2) At 70_{13} L has ܕܬ̈ܩܘܠ : problaby we should read ܕܢܓܠܬ݂ with P.

3) ܕܝܣܩܘܐܠܝܘܢ appears as a word in Payne Smith's *Thesaurus*, giving the reference "Pat.Vit." and quoting our text. "Pat.Vit." is explained as a MS used by Quatremère. It is evident therefore that E. M. Quatremère had read the Story of Euphemia from the Paris MS half a century ago for lexical purposes!

In the Greek we find *διδασκαλία*, but what is meant is a *διδασκαλικόν*, i.e. a document giving information about a case (*Labbé* IV 1641 B).

In view of emendations of dates proposed elswhere in this volume it is worth notice that 'seven' where it occurs in the narrative (58_9) is written out in full in L, but ܙ̄ in P.

2. *Agreements of* L 𝔊 *against* P.

§ 26 = 60_{5-6} Euphemia cries out in the tomb:

"Guria and Shmona and Habbib, *pillars and props of Edessa the Blessed*".

P omits the words in italics, but the Greek (176_1) has Σ. Γ. *καὶ* "Α., *στῦλοι καὶ ἀσφάλεια τῆσ πόλεώσ μου* 'Εδέσησ.

§ 31 = 62_{8-9} Euphemia begins her ejaculations of thans with:

"*All that the Lord willeth He doth in heaven and in earth*".

P omits these words, but they are in the Greek (180_7).

§ 33 = 63_6 The Custodian, hearing Euphemia's ejaculations, looked at her *marvelling* (ܒܗ̇. ܡܬܕܡܪ) according to L, but *in exasperation* (ܒܗ̇. ܡܬܡܪܡܪ) according to P. The Greek (180_{21}) has *ἐθαύμαζεν*. But for the Greek evidence we might have been tempted to regard the reading of P as original, as it is a rarer word, less obvious in the context, and yet capable of explanation, seeing that Euphemia was making a commotion and the Custodian had not yet heard her amazing story.

§ 34 = 64_{12} Euphemia tells her tale before her mother and *those that chaneed to be present* (ܐܝܠܝܢ ܕܐܬܩܪܝܘ).

10

P is much shorter, and the Greek quite paraphrastic, but the phrase ὥστε πάντασ τοὺσ παρατετυχηκότασ καὶ τῶν διηγηθέντων ἐπακούσαντασ θαυμάσαι (184_{12}) makes it clear that ܕܐܫܬܡܥܠܗ underlies it, and that therefore the longer reading of L is here original.

§ 35 = 66_4 The Goth comes back to Edessa, because of its enemies "the Persians, I mean, and the Huns, who had *agreed* to make war in this country". So L, but P has *were sent* instead of *agreed*. The Greek (186_{15}) has συμφωνησάντων γὰρ ..... Οὔννων τε καὶ Περσῶν, evidently supporting L.

3. *Agreements of* P 𝔊 *against* L.

§ 4 = 46_{2-4} P has "In the year 707 A.Gr. the Huns had come forth into the territory of the Romans, and they laid waste the country and captured many captives".

L has *Persians* for *Huns* (but on an erasure), omits *into the territory of the Romans* and transposes the final clauses. In agreement with P the Greek (150_6) has τὸ πονηρὸν ἔθνοσ καὶ ὀλέθριον, Οὖννοί φημι, ἐπελθόντεσ τοῖσ Ῥωμαϊκοῖσ μέρεσι καὶ πολλοὺσ καὶ διαφόρουσ τόπουσ πορθήσαντεσ καὶ πλείστην παραλαβόντεσ αἰχμαλωσίαν.

§ 24 = 58_{13} "The Goths devised to deliver Euphemia to the judge. And because the judge was far away, they" took her punishment into their own hands. So L. In P the Goths devised to deliver her to the judge, *and do many tortures upon her. And* the judge was far away, &c. This is inferior as literature: if Euphemia is to be brought to trial, her trial ought to come first before the sentence. But the extra clause is represented in the Greek (174_{3ff}): *ἐβούλοντο τοίνυν τῷ ἡγεμόνι ταύτην παραδοῦναι καὶ βασάνοισ πικραῖσ ὑποβαλεῖν καὶ οὕτω τῆσ παρούσησ ἐξεῶσαι ζωῆσ. τοῦ δὲ ἄρχοντοσ κεχωρισμένου κ.τ.λ.*

§ 37 = 69_1 Several clauses that are absent from L are added in P at the end of Sophia's speech to the Goth. The Greek (188_{16-18}) is very free, but the words *ἐν πολλῇ . . . . ὑπῆρχον φροντίδι* obviously correspond to **ܪ̈ܢܝܐ ܗ̇ܘܝܬ**, which are in P but not in L, so that the Greek supports the longer text here.

§ 39 = 69_{10} Here *ὀλολυγμοὺσ ἀναπέμψασα μετὰ πλείστησ ταραχῆσ ἐνεβριμήσατο* (190_{11}) corresponds to "cried out with a loud voice" (**ܐܝܒܒܬ**) in L, but "was agitated and wailed with a loud voice (**ܐܬܪܗܒܬ ܘܐܝܠܠܬ**) in P.

§ 44 = 73_5 The Stratelates asks the Goth how he dared to *bridle freedom with the yoke of slavery*, according to L. In P we find *bridle freedom with the cruel yoke of barbarian dominion.* The Greek (196_9) has *ἐλευθέραν κόρην ζυγῷ δουλείασ ὑποβέβληκασ ὑπὸ βάρβαρον καὶ φονικὴν δεσποτείαν*, or (as the inferior recension has it) *ἐλευθ. κόρην ζ. δουλ. βαρβάροισ ὑποβαλών.* Here again the Greek supports P against L, which seems to present an inferior paraphrase. It is worth notice that the variations between L and P have nothing to do with the variations between $\mathfrak{G}^A$ and $\mathfrak{G}^B$.

These examples will suffice to shew that L and P are independent of each other, and that the more primitive reading is found sometimes in one, sometimes in the other. As a rule the Greek version gives little help, being too paraphrastic. In § 15 = 52_2, however, σχῆμα δουλικόν points to ܠܒܘܫܐ ܕܐܡܗܘܬܐ in Syriac, lit. "garments of slave-girldom", i.e. "the costume of a slave-girl". Here L has ܕܐܪܡܠܘܬܐ "of widowhood", which is inappropriate; P has ܕܐܡܗܬܐ "of slave-girls", which is passable, but the scribe seems to have originally written something beginning with ܕܐܪ, so that P's final reading is probably only a clever emendation of what we find in L.

It should further be pointed out that in § 19 = 54_{14}, where L says that Euphemia's mistress treated her with "*great* hatred and *great* enmity", P presents us with "*much* hatred and enmity *without end*". Opinions may differ as to which is better style, but I think there is little doubt that ܪܒܬܐ .... ܪܒܬܐ would be more likely to be turned into ܕܠܐ ܣܘܦܐ .... ܣܓܝܐܬܐ than *vice versa*. We must therefore allow in P for conscious stylistic alterations.

Other inferior readings of P are to be found in § 2 = 45_2 [1]); § 4 = 46_9; § 19 = 55_8 (P adds ܦܠܠ); § 24 = 59_4; § 27 = 60_{10} [2]); § 29 = 61_3; § 31 = 61_{13} (for L, see Judges VI 21); § 35 = 65_{12}; § 36 = 66_{14}—67_4.

On the other hand, the whole address of Euphemia to the Confessors in § 17 = 53_{11-15} is more vigorous in the text of P, as well as shorter, than in that of L. Here however the Greek gives no textual help.

The comparative merits of L and P being so difficult to determine, I have thought it best to print L as it

1) *Haiklā* in later Syriac had the definite meaning of 'nave'.

2) Here possibly the Greek may induce us to combine L and P.

stands, only removing one or two slips of transcription, at the same time giving in the apparatus all the variants of P, so that any one may easily reconstruct an eclectic text as he pleases. I have not attempted to indicate the readings supported by the Greek, as it is in general so free and paraphrastic that its evidence could only be given by means of elaborate quotations. For convenience of reference, however, I have inserted in the margin the 46 chapters into which v. Dobschütz divides the narrative. They are not very suitable divisions for the Syriac text, as the Greek version makes many omissions in the less edifying parts of the tale, so that the chapters are of varying length and sometimes include distinct incidents.

This elaborate discussion of the Syriac text of *Euphemia* may appear somewhat disproportionate. My special reason for inserting it is to suggest to the imaginations of my readers how very much more serious the transmitted variants to *Shmona and Guria* and to *Ḥabbib* would have been, if we had not unfortunately been dependent for each of these important texts upon a single MS. We may roughly compare the 9th cent. MS of *Ḥabbib* in value to L, and the 15th cent. MS of *Shmona and Guria* to P. It is reassuring to find, in the case of *Euphemia*, that the later MS, though depraved in orthography and under some slight suspicion of having been here and there subjected to stylistic 'improvements', has nevertheless preserved in essentials the substance of the story and the general wording with which it was told centuries earlier [1]).

1) The two MSS which contain the story of Euphemia have recently

THE STORY OF EUPHEMIA.

The Story of the Holy Sophia and of Euphemia her daughter, 1
who were from the City of Edessa.

To-day it behoves us to sing with the spiritual prophet David "The Lord is nigh unto the broken in heart and the lowly in spirit doth He save", and again "The Lord is nigh unto them that call upon Him in truth, and doth good pleasure for them that fear Him". And the divine Apostle Paul teacheth us, saying "All your anxiety cast upon God, for He careth for you".

A miracle, then, that was performed in the blessed
city of Edessa some time ago do we announce before
you, O faithful brethren of ours, and sons of Holy 2
Church! A certain man, faithful and true and worthy
of good remembrance, and by rank a presbyter of the
clergy of the holy church there, at Edessa, who was
Paramonarius (i.e. Custodian) in the holy temple of the

Variants of the Paris MS (B. N. Syr. 234) = P.

Title in P: Item, the Story of Euphemia and Sophia her daughter, and of the Miracle that was performed for them by the Confessors Shmona and Guria (*Add. in mg.* and Ḥabbib) — their prayer be with us, Amen!

2 Ps XXXIV 19 3 Ps CXLV 18f. 5 good pleasure] *see Notes*, p. 183 6 Paul] P < 7 I Pet V 7 8 blessed] P < 9 announce] P repeat 10 brethren of ours, and] P < 11 and true] P < 12 and by rank] P < 13 there, at] P of 14 temple] P church

Shrine of the Confessors, — he transmitted to us the story of this miracle that came to pass in his days, as he learned from the mouth of the girl and her mother, after God had wrought deliverance for her and she had returned to her country and the home of her kindred by means of the help and power that dwells and abides at all times where lie the bones of the Holy ones and Confessors: this story, when that excellent old man heard it, he feared to hide and conceal and hold his peace about, and not to transmit to the generations that come after the deliverance of this great miracle, which by the working of the suretyship of those Martyrs and
3 Athletes, the Confessors, he heard and saw. And inasmuch as he trusted that with correctness he affirmed and spoke truth, he transmitted this story to us so that it might be possible that we should repeat it. And because the thing is simple and unphilosophical and the understanding of the old man weak, do not let the story of this wonderful thing be despicable in your eyes because of the simplicity of him who wrote it down.

4 In the year 707 by the reckoning of the Greeks [= 396 AD.] the Huns had come forth, and they cap-

1 he] P who 3 learned] P *pr.* had 6 power] P *pr.* divine

6—8 dwells .... Confessors] P is where lie the bones of the Holy ones, the true Confessors, and broods (there) at all times

8—10 this story .... about] P and this excellent old man was alarmed to conceal and hold his peace and hide it

10 generations] P + and to the ages

12—13 Martyrs .... Confessors] P victorious Athletes and Confessors

13—14 inasmuch as] P because

14—15 with correctness .... and] P <

18—19 the story .... thing] P this great miracle

20 simplicity .... down] P lowliness of the thing

22 Huns P (= *Gk*)] L Persians *in the mg.*, *and also in the text*, *but on an Erasure*: *see* pp. 52, 74

tured many captives and laid waste the country and they
came as far as Edessa. And Addai, the Military Governor
(Stratelates) at that time, did not give permission for
the *Foederati* to go out against them because of treachery in the midst, and for this cause the armies of
the Romans came down and lived in Edessa for a time.
Now a certain Goth of a fierce temper from that army 5
of the Romans was staying in a house, billeted upon a
certain believing widow whose name was Sophia, and
she had one virgin orphaned daughter, the only child
she had. And heedfully and carefully did her mother
keep her, and as was fitting she was bringing her up in
all modesty, and was keeping her close in hiding that
that wicked Goth should not see her. And as for the
girl herself, her name was Euphemia, and in her appearance she was very beautiful.

And when the Goth had been a long space of time 6
with them it fell out that for an instant he saw the girl
and was greatly inflamed with the desire of her, and
with the love of her his soul was taken captive; and 7
from then he began with soft and gentle words to
wheedle the mother of the girl to give him (as he said)

22—1 and they captured .... country] P into the territory of the Romans, and they laid waste the country and captured many captives
4 *Foederati*] i.e. the Gothic Mercenaries: *see Notes*, p. 184
6 time] P *pr.* long 7 Goth] P man 8 of the Romans] P < in a house .... upon] P with 10 one] P an only orphaned] P < 10—11 the .... had] P <
11—13 And .... hiding] P And her mother was heedful of her, and was bringing her up in all modesty, and was keeping her continually in hiding 15—16 and in .... beautiful] P and she, the girl, was beautiful 17—19 And when .... desire of her] P Now it chanced that he saw that girl and desired her 20 taken] P + away
21 from then] P < with ... words] P <
22 girl] P + with words (as he said)] P <

her daughter Euphemia in marriage to be his wife. But
her believing mother when she heard it was much agitated and was afraid of him, and did not accept his
suit. But that bad man did not cease from vexing her
with disturbing words in this wise, and sometimes it
was with fury that he met her, and sometimes with
8 words of gentleness and of flattery, and with mighty
oaths he was wheedling her, and displaying gold too
and shewing it before her, making pretexts in all manner
of ways that she should give him her free-born daughter.
9 Then she hid her daughter that he should not even
see her, saying to him "Man, what have I to do with thee? Why dost thou vex me, that am desolate and a widow, and cannot at all do this". But he was full of cunning in his guile and promised her many things.

But she said further to him: "And how can this be, seeing that thou hast, I do not know how many times over, a wife in thine own country and sons?" But the rogue insisted and swore, and ventured on oaths by God, falsely declaring "No wife at all have I taken nor have I got sons". And he brought the gold that he had displayed and put it before her, saying: "Lo, see that I have no wife; for lo, much gold for thy daughter have I displayed and many good things I will do for her".

1 to be his wife] P < 2—3 her believing .... and] P the believing woman 4 that bad] P the cease] P abstain 5 with .... this wise] P < 7 words .... and of] *om.* P 9—10 shewing .... ways] P made pretexts from all sides 11 Then] P But 12—13 what .... thee?] P < 13—14 P a widow and desolate 14 at all] P < was] P being 15 and promised] P when he promised (*sic*) 19—20 and ventured .... falsely] P < 20 at all] P < 22 Lo, see] P See 24 displayed] P *pr.* taken and

And again she said to him: "Man, why dost thou vex me? take thyself away from me". And he still made himself firm against her, mingling even oaths with flatteries.

And when he had greatly worn her out, and for 10
many days to this intent was vexing her, she was overcome like a weak woman and gave up opposition in
her mind, saying "God of the orphans and the widows,
come to my help! My God, this business is entrusted
to Thee, to whom alone it is revealed!" And it was a
greatly vexed question between the mother of the girl
and the Goth, she saying: "I cannot bear to let my
daughter be separated from me all this distance". But
he was swearing by God "I will not remove her from
thy side, and by thee we will settle".

And when the woman heard the oaths of the wicked 11
man, she was reconciled to fulfil his will, and then
forthwith they made a deed of dowry and she gave her
daughter in marriage.

And after a time God gave that there should be peace, and the order came that this wicked man should depart to his own country with the rest of the Goths that

1 And again she] P But the woman again 2 vex me] P + who am a solitary woman And] P But 2—3 made himself firm] P excited himself 3—4 mingling .... flatteries] P and was multiplying oaths 5—6 and for .... vexing her] P < 7—8 in her mind] P < 9 My God] P God this] P the
10 alone] P < 14 by God] P mighty oaths
14—15 "I .... settle"] P "If thou givest her to me, we will quickly come from our country, I and she, and we will both establish ourselves by thee" 16 And when] P Then when 16—17 the oaths .... man] P these mighty oaths 17 she .... his will] P she gave up opposition 17—18 then forthwith] P < 18 a deed] P deeds
gave] P + him 21 the order] P *pr.* when wicked] P audacious 22—3 with the rest .... And] P <

were with him, and it was arranged that Euphemia
also whom he had married he should take with him
12 where he was departing to. And her mother began to
affirm that this should never be, and that her daughter
should not go with him, because she was obviously
with child.

13 And when she had struggled much and many days
had raised a dispute over this, at the last she was overcome, and she could not save her daughter and keep
her behind from going with him.

And when it was decided about the separation of her
only child, she took the liar her son-in-law and her
daughter, and brought them up to the martyr-shrine of
the holy Confessors Guria and Shmona and Ḥabbib, and
they were praying, the mother with that daughter of
hers, with lamentable tears.

And when they had sealed their prayer with a tear
the mother of the girl drew near and took hold of her
by her right hand and set her upon the Coffin of the
Confessors themselves, saying to her false son-in-law
"Give me for a surety the hidden power that dwells on
these Holy Ones! Both thou dost know, and they do,
14 according as thou dost treat her!" But the blessed ones
themselves she exhorted, saying: "I beseech you, victorious saints of God, go with her and stand up for her
in the country of the stranger, for to God and to you

3 her] P the girl's 4 that this .... and] P < 7—12 And when .... only child] P And when she could not save her from him, and was overcome by him 15—16 with .... hers] P and her daughter 17 sealed .... tear] P prayed 20 Confessors] P *pr.* holy false] P lying 22 these Holy] P *pr.* the bones of 22—23 Both .... treat her] P Both thou and they — thou knowest, as thou dost deal with her (*sic*) 24—25 I .... God] P < 26—1 for .... behalf] P <

I trust on her behalf". And the Goth drew near and laid his hand and took her from the Coffin of the Holy ones, saying "As I deal with her and do unto her, so may God deal with me! Lo, these Holy ones are sureties that I will not grieve her!" And they all prayed, and they went down from thence, but her mother was in bitter sorrow and in constant weeping by night and by day that she was deprived of the care and the sight of her daughter.

And when the girl went off with that Goth and they 15
had gone many stages and had arrived at one stage off the city where they were going, then he rose up against her like a destroying wolf and stripped off her rich clothing that she was clothed with, and unloosed from her the gold with which she was festooned, and clothed her in the costume of a slave-girl. Then he revealed to her all the treachery he had practised on her, saying to her "I have a wife and I have married her, lo, this long while. But hold thy peace, and do not reveal before her or before any body else what has passed between us; otherwise an evil death thou wilt die at the hands of her family and tribesmen, for they are well known in our country".

And when the girl heard these things she sighed be- 16
fore God and lifted up her voice in her weeping, beating her face and her breast and scattering dust on her head

3 and do unto her] P < 4 sureties] P *pr.* my 5 all] P < 6 from thence] P < 8 deprived of] P separated from 10 And when] P But when 12 where .... going] P of the treacherous one then] P < 13—14 her rich clothing] P the rich clothes 16 costume of a slave-girl (= *Gk*)] Pcorr c. of slave-girls; L (P*?) clothes of widowhood: *see* p. 76 18 lo] P < 19 while] P + for years 22 her] P the woman's 25 her weeping] P < her

and on her face, and thus she was saying to him, the poor lonely thing, to that Goth, as she wept: "Thanks for thy kindness, man, for what thou hast done by me and by my state as a stranger here! Thanks for thy kindness, robber, stealing away freemen by day, that thou hast revealed to me that I am a slave-girl and hast fettered me with the yoke of slavery, and hast not killed me with drawn sword! These are thy promises! This is the covenant of thy oaths! Well, then, I will call to the sureties, that were between me and thee, and that mighty Power which is hidden in the bones of the Martyrs. Well, then, on the sureties that thou gavest me, what time thou stretchedst forth thy audacious hand and tookest me from them, do I cast my hope and on their Lord — beware what thou doest with me!"

17 And these things did the defrauded and lonely creature repeat in her prayer, as with lamentations she was weeping and saying: "God of my fathers, arise for me in the country of the stranger and save me and deliver me from the hands of this traitor that has rewarded me evil things for good and hatred for love! To you therefore I call, to the Confessors, my sureties! See the freedom fettered in the yoke of slavery! God, that didst accompany Joseph and wast a companion to him in the land of the Egyptians, turn not away Thine eyes

3 by me and] P < 5 by day,] P + Thanks for they kindness 8 drawn] P *pr.* thy 9—10 to the sureties] P to my sureties 10 mighty] P < 12—13 what time thou] P and 13 audacious] P treacherous 15 beware .... me] P see what he has done with me 16 And these] P These 17—18 as .... and] P and weeping with lamentation she was 21 things] P < 21—22 To you .... to the] P < 23—24 that didst .... to him] P that wast to Joseph a companion

from me! Thou carest, O my Lord, for the servitude of
freemen!"

And when they arrived and entered his house, that 18
wife of the Goth saw the girl that she was fair and
comely, and forthwith she was perturbed and agitated,
and began to ask her husband "Whence is this girl,
and what is her history? And what is her country, and
what is she doing with thee?" But that wicked one
said "She is thy slave, and I have brought her for thee
from Syria." And she answered and said to him: "Indeed
thou art lying, for her appearance is witness that she
is not like the slave-girls." And he again replied to her
"I tell the truth, that she is thy slave." Now the lonely 19
girl, when she saw what had befallen her, prepared herself to serve in slavery, while by night and by day she
was calling on God and saying only this: "My God, keep
not Thy help far from me! Holy Martyrs, rise up for me
in the land of the stranger! Confessors, my sureties, see
my servitude and judge judgement for my oppression!"

Now her mistress used to speak with great hatred and
great enmity to her, and was using her with indignity
and boxing her ears continually. And the girl did not

2 freemen!] P + Confessors! from you he took me, and in you my mother confided! 3 they] P he that] P and the
4—5 and comely] P < 5 and] P <
10 she answered and] P again she 11 is witness that she] P <
12 like] P + that of P
12—13 And .... slave"] P But he was cavilling "she is thy slave"
13 lonely] P <
14—15 prepared .... serve in] P subjected herself to
16 calling on God] P weeping much
16—17 My God .... far from me] P <
17 Holy Martyrs] P Confessors, my sureties
20 great hatred] P much hatred
21 great enmity] P enmity without end to her] P to the girl

18

know how to speak in her language or to appeal to her about anything, but only was weeping with sighing and calling the Confessors to her help; for she was longing for somebody to speak Syriac with her, and there was no one but that Goth who had taken her away from the Syrian country, as from the length of time he had been in Edessa he had learnt to speak. And when the Goth woman had seen that the girl was with child she did not spare her, but all the more put additional hard work upon her and was demanding of her more than her strength, so that in one way or another she should end her life.

20 And when the days had come near for the girl to bear, there was born to her a man-child, and he was like his father exceedingly; and when the wife of the Goth saw that the baby was like her husband she was struck with envy, and in great indignation she said to her husband: "Look and see how like he is to thee! Here therefore cavilling and lying are of no use to thee!" And when many times in indignation she had said this to him, he saith to her: "Thou hast authority over her; everything thou dost wish to do, do, for she is thy slave."

21 Now this companion to Jezebel the murderess of the Prophets covered her self with zeal against the boy and took thought to kill it, and she brought out some

1 in her language] P with her in the language
2—3 with sighing .... help] P < 3 for] P and
6 the Syrian country] P her country length of] P <
7 speak] P + a little 11 more] P *pr.* to do
13 And when] P Now when 14 and he] P who
16 her husband] P his father 17 therefore] P <
22 for] P < 24 Now] P Then 25 zeal] P envy

murderous deadly poison that when there was opportunity she might make the baby lick it and he should die, for she was exceedingly troubled by the sight of him. And on one of the days when the baby was crawling along it cuddled up against her supposing that she was its mother, and threw itself upon her; and she forthwith became exceedingly embittered and sent its mother away to market, to a place a long way off, on some excuse or other. And when she saw that its mother was not near, she took that deadly poison and made the boy, or rather baby, lick it; and when the baby's mother 22
came from where her mistress had sent her she sees her son in a fit: and some of that deadly poison had been vomited up and it was congealed on the baby's lips! And say anything she could not, but only weep bitterly and call on the Confessors to her help. And she devised in her heart and brought a lock of wool and wiped from the lips of her son that deadly poison which the Goth woman had made him lick, and she laid it in her handkerchief and kept it with care.

And after a little while the boy died and was buried.

And a little time after the decease of the son of the 23
lonely and oppressed girl there was a supper made by the Goth, and his friends were invited. And in the evening, when it was dark, she found a moment favourable to do by her mistress what she had done by her son, and that her wickedness should return on her own head,

5 supposing] P and supposed 7 its] P the baby's
11 boy or rather] P < 14 the baby's] P his
15 only] P < 20 handkerchief] P pillow care] P *pr.* great
21 after .... while] P <
25 she] P the girl favourable] P + for her

and in the snare that she that she had hidden she might be caught even to the death. So when she was serving them as a maid and was mixing drink for them, the lock of wool with which she had wiped the lips of her son she took out from her handkerchief and dipped it in the cup of wine, saying: "I shall see whether she made my son lick anything that he died: and if not, I shall know that it was by a death from God that my son died."

And when she devised this, she mixed the cup and gave it to the Goth's wife; and when her mistress took and drank that cup she too slept a deadly slumber, and in the pit that she digged, in it she fell. And the Goth's wife died and was buried.

24 And after seven days of mourning for her the family and kindred of the Goth woman woke up like lions, and the thought came over them that the stranger girl had given her the cup of deadly poison that she died of, and they devised against her to deliver her up to the judge. And because the judge was far from that place, the counsel approved itself to their heart that they should bind her in the tomb by the stinking corpse and should shut the door in her face. And while they were dragging her along and beating her the people of

1—2 she might be] P she herself was
5 from her handkerchief] P < 9 my son] P he
12 and drank that cup] P that cup from the girl and drank
13 the pit] P + of death P 15 seven] P "7"
17 girl] P slave-girl 18 deadly poison] P death 20 the judge (1°)] P + and do many tortures upon her because] P <
21 the counsel .... heart] P and further the thought approved itself to them.
22 tomb] P + of her mistress 23 And while] L* < And
24 dragging her along] P making shipwreck of her

the city saw her, and they were grieved for her. And after they had gone and bound her in the tomb by the corpses they took thought lest the people of the city should come and open for her and let her out, and they rolled a great and mighty stone and laid it at the door of it, so that no one should be able to roll the stone from the tomb. And they took thought further that hard by the tomb they would sleep all that night, and in the early morning they would take her out from the tomb and impale her on a stake and shoot at her with arrows, because the judge was far from that place.

And when they were hearing the sound of her weeping and her anguish they had no pity for her. Now the smell of the stink of that corpse grew more stifling and was killing her.

Then she cried out in prayer unto God and said: 25
"God of Guria and of Shmona and of Ḥabbib! God,
for the truth of whose faith Thy Holy ones the Confessors gave their necks to the slaughter, God that didst
receive their blood as a living and holy sacrifice, come
to the help of Thy handmaiden! God that for sinners
didst mount the Cross of shame, deliver me from this
distress! Guria and Shmona and Ḥabbib, pillars and 26
props of Edessa the Blessed, quickly let your help over-
take me! My sureties the Confessors, aid me in this hour!"
Then God heard her cry and her supplication, and 27

1 the city] P that city
2—3 by the corpses] P with the corpse
3—4 they took .... for her] P the people of the city had taken thought to come and open the tomb
6 able] P + at all 6—7 roll the stone from] P open
17 and of .... and of] P and .... and
23—24 pillars .... Blessed] P <

of a sudden the fierce and stinking smell of the stench
of the corpse was turned to a pleasant smell of spices,
and in the likeness of three men they appeared to her
with a great light, saying to her: "Fear not, Euphemia;
we are with thee and we will not leave thee! Quickly
comes thy deliverance, for our bond is near to be ful-
filled, and the faith of thy fathers is not to be oppressed."
28 And there fell upon her a slumber and she slept, and
29 by the Power to which everything is easy this unspeak-
able miracle was wrought for her, as also unto the Prophet Habakkuk in his time, in that when Daniel was
hungry while he was lying in the midst of the den of
lions in Babylon a meal from Jerusalem by the hand
of Habakkuk was sent to him: so also, by the Divine
Power that resides in the bones of the holy Martyrs
and Confessors to whom she called and in whom she
had taken refuge, in that very night she found herself
on the hill by the side of the Shrine of the holy Mar-
30 tyrs and Confessors. And when the East shewed, she
felt stupefied as if from sleep, and she saw the holy
Martyr Mar Shmona in the likeness of an old man
standing by her, and saying to her: "Dost thou know
where thou art now, and where thou art standing?"
But she lifted up her eyes and saw the holy Shrine of
the Confessors, and as now the sun was risen she went

1 and stinking] P < 2 of spices] P that were (*sic*) beyond price
9 this] P an 12 the midst of] P <
16 and Confessors] P the Confessors
16—17 to whom .... refuge] P to whom she drew near
17 herself] P that she was 18 on the hill] P + of Edessa
18—19 P the Martyr-shrine of the holy Confessors
21 Mar (= My Lord)] P <
25 as .... risen] P just while the sun was rising went] P goes

to enter the holy Shrine of the Martyrs. Saith the blessed Shmona to her: "Lo, our bond is paid: go in peace!" And immediately he vanished from her, and she looked 31
to the right and to the left and in every direction, but she saw him no more.

And when she came to the door of the Shrine of the Martyrs, she heard the usual service, and she was filled with great joy and fear, and she was astonished and as in a dream she was seeing the affair. For the Proper Psalm for them was "With my voice unto God I called, and He heard me; and I lifted up with my voice unto Him, and He answered me. In the day of my distress I sought the Lord." And her heart rejoiced, and exceedingly was she cheered with these words of the service that they were performing. And she had drawn near by the Coffin of the Holy ones, the Confessors, and cast herself before them and with much weeping she was saying "All that the Lord willeth He doth in heaven and in earth, that in the evening should be weeping and in the morning joy, for He hath sent from heaven and delivered me. Blessed be Thy Glory from Thy Place, O Lord, of whose praises heaven and earth are full! Blessed is the habitation of Thy Holy ones — your bond is paid, holy Confessors! Blessed is the Power of your Lord, that doth dwell in your bones! No one that taketh

1 holy] P < 3 vanished] P disappeared
8 astonished] P astonishment (*sic*) 9 For the] P The
10 Ps LXXVII 1 f. 13 exceedingly] P <
18—19 All .... earth (Ps CXXXV 6)] P <: *see* p. 73
19 for that in (Ps. XXX 6)] P In should be] P <
22 O Lord] P <
23 Thy Holy] P the Holy
23—24 — your .... Confessors!] P <
25 dwell in] P dwell upon

refuge in you is ashamed! No one that doth flee to your shelter and run unto you is vanquished! I confess to you, the oppressed slave-girl that hath been set free; I confess to you, the captive that hath returned to her country! For lo, in the evening I was at a great distance in the city of the Goth a captive, and now I am in the blessed City of Edessa, in the temple where lie your bones, my sureties and my saviours and my deliverers from them that were distressing me. Holy is your habitation and adorable is the Power that resides in you!"

32 And when she had said these things, and lamentable tears from her eyes on the Coffin of the Holy ones she was shedding, the custodian was looking at her marvelling, and when they finished the service he drew near unto her and was asking her and saying: "Woman, why art thou agitated, and what is thy business?" But the believing one repeated before him all the deed that God had done by her from the beginning even unto the end.

33 And when the custodian heard these things, he was astonished at the greatness of the matter so as even to doubt, and he sought to be assured of the truth and he wished to learn the abode of her mother, and with much diligence he sent and brought her mother that he might learn from her whether the matter was as her daughter said.

Now when her mother heard, forthwith she was much agitated, for that she supposed that she and her husband

1 in you] P with you 2 and run unto you] P <
6 now] P + in the morning 9 them .... me] P my distresses
10 and adorable .... in you] P < 11 lamentable] P urgent
13 marvelling] P in exasperation 15 and saying] P <
17 the deed (*lit.* 'business')] P miracle
25 said] P + to him 26 forthwith] P <

had come. But when her mother had come up to the Shrine of the blessed Martyrs the Confessors she saw her daughter and did not recognise her for that she was clothed with garments of humiliation; but her daughter recognised her, her mother, and drew near and did obeisance to her.

Now when her mother recognised that it was her daughter, the minds of the two of them were stirred with love and affection, and they were embracing each other and they could not speak with one another for much weeping.

34 And when they had been much time thus, the brethren of the Shrine of the Martyrs gathered together, and every one that was found there at the Shrine of the Martyrs was amazed at the weeping that was holding the two. Then the Custodian asked Euphemia to tell before her mother the tale she had told before him and she told before her mother and before those that chanced to be present the tale of what the Divine Power that dwells in the bones of the holy Martyrs the Confessors had done unto her, and how the Holy ones had taken her forth from the tomb that she was bound in and brought her many stages in the night. And every one that heard gave thanks and praised God, who doth the pleasure of them that fear Him. Now her mother sent

4 garments of humiliation] P humble garments
7 recognised] P + her daughter and knew
15—16 that was holding the two] P of the two
16 Then (P *and* L corr vid)] L* But she
18—19 before (1°) .... of what] P everything that
20 in] P upon holy] P <
21 the Holy ones] P they
24—25 doth the pleasure of] P doth good pleasure for *(change of one letter)*: *see Note on* § 1

19

and brought for her garments to put on and they stayed there all that day.

But when the sun drew near to set, they went down to their houses giving thanks to God, for the abundance of His grace that He had done by them. Now after the day was over the tale of this affair had gone forth in all the city, and her family and the people of her neighbourhood gathered together; and when they saw her, they rejoiced and gave thanks to God who doth not neglect those that worship Him. And while the women were staying together they were constant in prayer in the House of God, but on Sunday and on Friday they used to go up always and stay all day before the Coffin of the holy Martyrs in all modesty.

35 And after a little time that mighty Power of our Creator, which is not be spoken or explained, shewed its vengeance as it is wont, and justice was aroused upon that wicked and lying man, the Goth; and by the Providence of God that was in this business the Goth came against his will to Edessa again with a certain General who had been sent by the Emperor to this place to keep it from the enemies, the Persians, I mean, and the Huns, who had agreed to make war in this country. And as Pharaoh was caught in the Red Sea, so also this Goth was caught in the snare that he had hidden,

1 brought] P *pr.* they 2 all] P < 3 sun] P day
4 houses] *see* p. 147[16] 5—6 Now .... over] P And after that day
7 the people] P *pr.* all 10 And] P <
11 together] P < they] P and
12—13 but .... stay] P and on Friday and on Sunday they did not cease from going up and staying
15—16 of our Creator] P that is in them
20 again] P < 22 I mean] P <
23 agreed] P been sent 25 this] P that snare] P *pr.* very

and the Lord returned to him his recompence upon his head, and the pit that he digged, in it he fell, and in the net that he had hidden was he taken that despised the oaths and had contempt for the suretiship of the holy Martyrs, and trembled not at the fearful judgement of God. And Justice herself impelled him that in the very 36
place that he had despised the oaths and lied he should receive the punishment of requital for his treachery.

And (so) on one of the days, when he, the Goth, was walking in the market, a certain man, their neighbour, saw him and spake with him, and he, the wicked and guilty fellow, just as if he did not know him or recognise him passed by him in agitation and did not linger for him, nor did he speak with him, but overlooked him as if not knowing him. And at once direct to the houses of Sophia and of Euphemia did that man, their neighbour, go up to let them know about that man, the Goth, and he was saying to them "That treacherous and guilty fellow who did by you all that treachery and great evil — to-day I have seen him and spoken with him. But contrive and see how it is fitting that this affair should be done."

Then forthwith they gathered together all their neigh-

1 to him] P < recompence] P wickedness
5 trembled .... God] P his heart trembled not
6 very] P < 7 he should] P *pr.* in it 8 of] P and
9 he, the Goth] P that wicked Goth
10 their neighbour] P one of their neighbours
11—15 and he .... knowing him] P for so agitated was the guilty Goth, that he neither recognised him nor lingered for him and spoke with that man as he should have spoken, but overlooked him and spoke with him in agitation and did not linger for him
16 houses (LP*)] P[corr] house 17—18 to let .... Goth] P to make that Goth known 19 that treachery and] P this
23 Then forthwith they] P Now they forthwith

bours and their relations, and this they thought to do, that no one should reveal to him that her daughter Euphemia had come to this country. And all her kin went forth to seek that Goth with diligence; and when they found him they spake with him in friendliness, saying to him "In thy mother-in-law's house it were fitting that thou shouldest stay and rest, and thither it were right that thou go directly, because she is in much cogitation about thee and very desirous to see thee about her daughter." And having flattered him they brought him up to the house of Sophia his mother-in-
37 law. But she, that faithful woman Sophia, had shut up Euphemia her daughter in an inner chamber, that he might not see her at present, so that all his falsehood and his treachery that he had done by them might be exposed.

And when her neighbours and her relations had gathered together against the man in the midst of the house, Sophia his mother-in-law began to ask him, the liar, saying "What is thy tale, my son? And what is the tale of Euphemia my daughter? How did the journey treat you? Has a son been born to you? Is it a boy or

2 to him] P + to that Goth her daughter] P thy daughter
4 went forth .... diligence] P used great diligence to seek that Goth
7 fitting] P + for thee 7—8 and rest .... go] P <
10 about her daughter] P and ask thee about her having flattered him] P exhibiting much love for him they wheedled and flattered him (*sic*)
11—12 Sophia .... -law] P Euphemia 12 woman] P <
13 Euphemia] P < that he] P so that the Goth
14 so that] P *pr.* and
15 them (*fem.*)] P them (*masc.*)
17 P their neighbours and all her relations
19 the liar] P < 20 saying] P + to him tale] *lit.* 'voice' my son] P <
22 Is it] P <

a girl? For I have been much in anxiety about you,
because of the length of the journey!"

Now the treacherous fellow opened his mouth in false- 38
hood and said to her: "In health we travelled, in peace
the whole way; and we entered our city in tranquillity
and joy, and we have no evil tale and we are in health.
And thy daughter sends greeting to thee and her most
dutiful reverence for thee, and no hurt at all hath she,
and a son hath been born to us, a boy, — and may
all those that thou lovest among your family be like
her! And if we had not come forth hastily from our
country, with me she was ready to come to see thee."

And when Sophia heard these words of falsehood 39
from that Goth, she trembled and rent her clothes, and
cried out with a loud voice and said "What has he done
to my daughter, the treacherous and lying fellow? These
are thy oaths! This is the covenant that thou has cove-
nanted with me! The sureties thou gavest me, they shall
bring thy life to an end, treacherous one!" And when 40
she said these things she brought out her daughter
Euphemia and set her before him, saying to him "Thou
knowest her, this girl here? Thou knowest how ye bound
her? Those sureties thou gavest me, they brought her
to me; the victorious Confessors, guardians of our country,
they brought her back from Sheol beneath, those holy

2 because .... journey] P for having let my daughter cross over. And how have you gone forth from thence? And for this I was grieving, because the journey was lengthy for you to go, that this might not happen to her, to my daughter, from the fatigue of the journey

4 in peace] P *pr.* and 5 city] P country

7 greeting] P *pr.* much 10 all those] P every one

12 ready to come] P coming here

15 cried out] P was agitated and wailed has he] P hast thou

16 the .... fellow] P < 25 back] P + to me

Martyrs, that thou didst stretch forth thy treacherous right hand and took her from, they rescued her from the tomb in which ye bound her living; Guria and Shmona and Ḥabbib became for her swift steeds and delivered her from your hands!"

41 Now he when he heard these things and saw the girl too — the colour of his face was changed, and like a dead man so he became, and he was silenced and could not open his mouth and return any answer for shame and for the fear and terror that fell upon him. And all they that were there seized that Goth, having bound him in the house in the midst of the house and they were all keeping watch over him. And they made an affidavit of all the affair, as it was from the beginning even to the end, and how with these many oaths and with great promises and with a deed of dowry he had taken the girl, swearing that he had not taken a wife in his own country, and how he had gone forth and given them for sureties the Confessors, the victorious Martyrs, and how he stretched out his right hand and took her from the Coffin where lie the bones of the holy Martyrs Shmona and Guria and Ḥabbib; and how they appeared to her when bound in the tomb shining with a great light and glory, and abolished the stinking

2 right] P < 4 swift steeds] *see* p. 62
7—8 like .... became] P became like a dead man
9 shame] P *pr.* his
10 the fear] P his fear terror] P *pr.* the
11 P the man, that Goth having] P and
12—13 and they were] P < 14 affidavit] *see* p. 72
15 these] P < 20 right] P <
22 Martyrs] P < 23 when bound in] P in the midst of
24 great] P splendid light and glory] P and glorious light abolished] P *pr.* it

smell of the corpse, for that there blew from them a sweet smell of spices; and how they brought her in one night the many stages.

And they went down and made it known to the chaste and holy priest Eulogius the Bishop, and they gave him the affidavit. Now the priest, when what was written was read before him, was astonished, yea, he marvelled at the audacity of that man, and great zeal was stirred 42
in him, yea, he undertook the care of this business. And he gathered together his clergy with the presbyter, the Paramonarius of the Shrine of the holy Martyrs, the Confessors, and unto His Excellency the Stratelates he went and made it known, that which was written in the affidavit having been read before him, just as the whole business was. Now the Stratelates and every one that was there when they heard were amazed thereat, at this great miracle, which God had wrought by the suretiship of the Confessors, the sureties and Victorious ones, and they marvelled how that Goth had been so bold and had not trembled.

Then the Stratelates in a rage gave orders and they 43
brought that Goth from where he was bound by them, and also the girl herself, Euphemia, and when they came they made them stand before the Stratelates and before

1 for that] P and   2 sweet] P <
4 went down] P came   5 Eulogius] P *pr.* Mar: *see* p. 142[21]
6 the priest] P he, the priest of God   7 yea, he] P and
9 yea] P and   10 his] P *pr.* all   13 he] P and they (*sic*)
13—14 that .... having been] P and when .... was (*sic*)
16 were] P was (*sic*)
18 the Confessors .... ones] P the Martyrs, the Confessors
21 rage] P *pr.* great   22 where] P the place that
23 herself] P <
24 they made] P he made   the Stratelates] P *pr.* His Excellency

the glorious and holy priest Eulogius the Bishop; and all the city was gathered together. And they gave orders that what was written in the affidavit should be read, that the Goth and the girl might hear. And as soon as it was all read, they asked the Goth and said to him "Is it true what thou hast heard written in this affidavit?" Now the Goth replied "Yea, my Lord, it is true, and there is no word of falsehood in it, not one!"

44 Then the Stratelates said to him "Oh audacious against the truth! how was it thou didst not tremble at the just judgement of God? And didst also be contemptuous of the pure laws of the Romans, and didst despise the oaths, yea make nothing of the covenant of the suretiship of the holy Martyrs, and give to subjection and bridle a free person with the yoke of slavery?" And forthwith the Stratelates commanded that he should receive sentence of execution by the sword and be burned with fire, for that he had dared to accomplish all this evil.

45 Now the true and merciful priest Eulogius the Bishop had entreated that it should not be for him so, but that with mercy he should use him. And when Eulogius had made much entreaty, the Stratelates replied to him: "I tremble to have mercy on this man, lest on me the

1 glorious and holy priest] P priest of God Eulogius] P *pr.* Mar
2 they] P he
7 Goth] P *pr.* wicked replied] P made reply and said
9—10 Oh .... truth!] P In truth tremble] P + audacious one
11 just] P < 13 yea] P and
15 a free person] *lit.* freedom yoke] P *pr.* cruel slavery] P barbarian dominion
16 commanded] P *pr.* fiercely 17 of .... sword] P <
18 all this] P this great 19 Eulogius the Bishop] P <
20 had entreated] P entreated him 21 Eulogius] P *pr.* the holy
22 replied] P made reply

Confessors should wreak vengeance, as one who con-
temns and as one who despises their suretiship, and that
others again should dare and should accomplish something like this fellow, trusting for mercy." Then they 46
led him and took him out of the city, and the sentence
of the sword he received, and because of much entreaty
he was exempted from the burning. And every one
glorified and praised God, who doth the pleasure of them
that fear Him and heareth and receiveth the supplication
of those that frequent His Gate and take refuge with
His Saints. To whom be glory and thanksgiving and
exaltation, and to the Father who sent Him for our
salvation, and to the Living and Holy Spirit, for ever
and ever, Amen.

Here endeth the story about S. Euphemia and about Sophia the mother of her, who were from Edessa the Blessed City.

1 Confessors] P Holy ones contemns] P looks askance at
2 as one who] P <
3—4 something .... fellow] P again something like this
7 the burning] P *pr.* the fire and
8 doth the pleasure of] P doth good pleasure for: *see Note on* § 1
11—12 and exaltation] P < 13 Living and] P <
13—14 for ever .... Amen.] P now (*i. e.* now, and for ever, *etc.*)

Subscription in P: Here endeth the story of the Miracle that the holy Confessors performed on Euphemia who was betrothed to the Goth in the City of Edessa. Now it was copied from an old book that was written in the Imperial City of Constantinople by John the Recluse Monk.

NOTES TO EUPHEMIA.

Most of the observations that I had to make upon *Euphemia* will be found above, pp. 70—77 for the text, and pp. 48—65 for the subject matter. I add here four detached observations for which no other satisfactory place offered itself.

§ 1 (Page 129, l. 5), also § 34 (Page 145, l. 24) and § 46 (Page 153, l. 8): see Syriac text ܩܟܛ 6, ܩܡܗ 16, ܩܢܓ 5.

In these three places we have evidently the same Syriac phrase. There is no variant in § 1: both L and P have ܥܒܕ ܨܒܝܢܐ ܠܕܚ̈ܠܘܗܝ and this is also the text of P in § 34 and § 46. But both in § 34 and in § 46 L has ܕܕܚ̈ܠܘܗܝ for ܠܕܚ̈ܠܘܗܝ, thereby assimilating the phrase to the Peshiṭta text of Psalm CXLV 19. The Greek gives no help: in § 1 it follows the Greek Psalter (θέλημα τῶν φοβουμένων αὐτὸν ποιήσει) and paraphrases in § 34 and § 46.

There can be little doubt that the reading of P is to be preferred, and that the scribe of L was influenced by the familiar words of the Psalm. For the idiom see the Life of Simeon Stylites (*Assemani* II 340 = *Bedjan* IV 611): Elijah prayed and the Lord "did for him a pleasure". Other examples are collected in Payne Smith, *s.v.* ܨܒܝܢܐ.

§ 1 (Page 129, l. 6 f.) *The quotation from* 1 Peter V 7. This quotation occurs in both Syriac MSS and agrees verbally with the Peshiṭta: short as it is, it contains a reading found nowhere but in Syriac, *viz.* the substitution of 'God' for 'He'. It is assigned in L to 'the divine Apostle Paul', but P knows better and leaves the name of Paul out. The whole quotation is omitted in the Greek, probably because the unfamiliar reading 'God' together with the mistaken ascription to 'Paul' made the passage unidentifiable to the translator.

As explained above, p. 57, it is hardly possible to date the first writing down of *Euphemia* before the death of Rabbula (435), and by that time the present Peshiṭta New Testament, which included 1 Peter, was well established in Edessa. But perhaps a trace of the comparative unfamiliarity to Syriac ears of this part of new the Canon may be detected in the substitution of 'Paul' for 'Peter'.

§ 4 (Page 131, l. 4) *The Foederati.* The Syriac is ܒܐܬܝܐ (so L): P reads ܒܐܬ̈ܝܐ, i.e. a plural, but the word is a transliteration of *βοήθεια*, and the only other passage where it seems to occur in Syriac supports the singular. This passage is *Bedjan* III 298_{16} (Sergius and Bacchus): the prisoners were to be transported from one city to another ܒܒܘܐܬܝܐ ܕܛܟܣܝܣ, by a *βοήθεια* of the *τάξισ*. What this means in technical language is not very easy to say; the ancient Latin version (*Acta SS.* for Oct. 7) says *per singula officia ciuitatum.* My colleague Professor Bury tells me that the *τάξισ* would be the staff of a provincial Governor, and also referred me to the use of Γοτθικὴ *βοήθεια* in Malalas (e.g. 369 and 374).

In 369 we read that the Governor of Antioch sent a *Γοτθικὴ βοήθεια* to fetch the corpse of Simeon Stylites.

From the context in *Euphemia* § 4 it is evident that the ܒܐܬܐ (Βοήθεια) was composed of Goths in Roman pay. The word is not used by Joshua Stylites. As noticed on p. 52, the Greek altogether leaves out this reference to Byzantine military organization.

§ 41 (Page 150, l. 22 = Syriac text ܟܐ 5). The three names *Shmona* and *Guria* and *Ḥabbib* are here vocalized in L

ܫܡܘܢܐ ܘܓܘܪܝܐ ܘܚܒܝܒ

This apparently indicates a pronunciation

Shmūnā, Gūrya, Ḥa(b)bīv.

On the forms in which *Ḥabbib* appears in Greek, see *v. Dobschütz*, p. 230. The other two Saints become Σαμωνᾶς and Γουρίας. It is clear from Syriac poetry that both *Shmona* and *Guria* (*Gur-ya*) are each words of two syllables, not of three, but so far as I know there is very little direct evidence to determine whether the first syllable was pronounced *o* or *u*. According to the Jacobite system of vocalisation every *o* becomes *u*, so that no help could be looked for from Codex P. The Greek evidence and L agree as to G*u*ria, but they appear to differ as to Shm*o*na (-*u*na). I do not know with what vowel ܫܡܘܢܝ, the mother of the seven Maccabaean Martyrs (2 Macc VII), ought to be pronounced.

والله اعلم

24

INDEX.

ܕܐܝܟ ܗܢܐ ܢܣܒܪܘܢ. ܟܕ ܡܬܬܟܠܝܢ ܥܠ ܡܪܚܡܢܘܬܐ.
46 ܚܕܝܢ ܕܒܪܘܗ̇ܝ، ܘܐܦܩܘܗ̇ܝ، ܠܒܪ ܡܢ ܡܕܝܢܬܐ. ܘܠܓܒܪ
ܕܝܢܐ ܕܚܫܘܟܐ ܩܒܠ. ܘܡܛܠ ܦܘܪܫܐ ܘܚܠܡܐ ܐܬܦܫܩܢ
ܡܢ ܢܟܪܝܐ. ܘܟܠܗ ܥܡܐ ܐܘܕܝ، ܠܐܠܗܐ ܕܥܒܕ ܢܝܫܐ
ܕܕ̈ܚܠܘܗ̇ܝ.. ܘܫܒܚ ܘܩܒܠ ܒܥܘܬܐ ܕܐܝܠܝܢ ܕܠܬܪ̈ܬܝܗ
ܢ̈ܦܫܢ ܘܒܡܕ̈ܝܢܬܗ، ܡܬܬܟܫܦܝܢ. ܕܠܗ ܫܘܒܚܐ ܘܬܘܕܝܬܐ
ܘܪܘܡܪܡܐ ܘܠܐܝܩܪܐ ܕܫܠܝܛܗ ܠܥܘܠܡܝܢ. ܘܠܥܠܡܐ ܐܡܝܢ
ܘܡܕܝܢܐ ܠܥܠܡ ܥܠܡܝܢ ܐܡܝܢ. ⁘ ܫܠܡܬ ܬܫܥܝܬܐ ܕܥܠ
ܡܪܝܫܬܐ ܐܘܦܡܝܐ. ܘܥܠ ܫܘܫܢܐ ܐܡܗ̇ ܕܝܠܗ̇..
ܗ̈ܢܝܢ ܕܡܢ ܐܘܪܗܝ، ܡܕܝܢܬܐ ܡܒܪܟܬܐ..

1 ܗܢܐ] P ܗܕܐ
4 ܢܟܪܝܐ] P *pr.* ܢܘܪܐ ܘ
5 ܕܕ̈ܚܠܘܗ̇ܝ] P ܠܕ̈ܚܠܘܗ̇ܝ
7 ܘܪܘܡܪܡܐ] P <
7, 8 ܐܡܝܢ ܘ] P <
8 ܠܥܠܡ ... ܐܡܝܢ.] P ܗܫܐ

Subscription in P

ܫܠܡܬ ܬܫܥܝܬܐ ܕܬܕܡܘܪܬܐ ܕܣܦܪܘ ܡܪ̈ܬܐ ܡܗ̈ܝܡܢܐ
ܒܐܘܦܡܝܐ ܕܐܬܡܪܬ ܠܓܘܬܐ ܒܐܘܪܗܝ، ܡܕܝܢܬܐ:
ܐܬܬܪܓܡܬ ܕܝܢ ܡܢ ܟܬܒܐ ܒܬܘܣܐ ܕܐܬܟܬܒ ܒܡܕܝܢܬ
ܩܠܬܐ ܩܘܣܛܢܛܝܢܘܦܘܠܝܣ ܡܢ ܝܘܢܝܐ ܕܝܢܐ ܣܒܝܣܐ

ܚܙܐ ܀ ܗܝܕܝܢ ܐܡܪ ܠܗ ܐܘܪܝܠܠܝܢܘܣ. ܡܪܝܐ ܒܨܪܝܐ: 44
ܐܝܟ ܠܐ ܐܚܕܬ ܗܘ ܕܝܢܐ ܒܐܝܕܐ ܕܐܠܗܐ. ܘܐܦ ܥܠ
ܢܦܫܐ ܕܟܝܐ ܕܐܘܦܡܝܐ ܒܛܘܪܬ: ܘܫܠܛܬ ܡܘܬܐ
ܐܦ ܫܠܛܬ ܥܡܟܐ ܕܛܪܘܬܐ ܕܥܡܕܐ ܡܕܝܢܐ ܘܡܢܥܬ
ܘܥܒܕܬ ܘܟܕܢܬ ܫܐܘܪܬܐ ܒܢܝܪܐ ܕܥܒܕܘܬܐ. ܘܡܫܝܕܐ
ܦܩܕ ܗܘܐ ܐܘܪܝܠܠܝܢܘܣ ܕܢܬܪܕܝܢܐ ܕܚܝܦܐ ܢܣܒ
ܘܒܝܘܪܐ ܢܐܡܪ. ܥܠ ܕܐܡܪܬ ܘܡܪܕ ܥܠܘܗ ܒܢܝܬܐ
ܗܕܐ ܀ ܗܘ ܕܝܢ ܒܗܝܢܐ ܥܕܪܐ ܘܡܪܚܡܢܐ ܐܘܠܒܢܘܣ 45
ܐܦܣܩܘܦܐ. ܐܦܝܣ ܗܘܐ ܕܠܐ ܢܗܘܐ ܠܗ ܗܘ ܗܟܢܐ.
ܐܠܐ ܒܡܪܚܡܢܘܬܐ ܢܬܚܫܚ ܠܬܘܗ. ܘܟܕ ܫܦܠ ܐܦܝܣ
ܗܘܐ ܐܘܠܒܢܘܣ: ܥܠ ܠܗ ܐܘܪܝܠܠܝܢܘܣ. ܕܢܐܬܐ ܐܢܐ
ܐܪܝܟ ܥܠ ܟܪܣܐ ܗܢܐ. ܕܐܠܗܐ ܐܦ ܗܘ ܢܦܩܘܕ
ܦܘܩܕܢܐ ܢܣܥܬܐ ܐܝܟ ܘܐܝܟ ܡܨܡܪܢܐ ܥܘܠܐ
ܕܛܪܝܒܘܬܗܘܢ ܘܠܐ ܬܘܒ ܢܦܪܘܩ ܐܢܫܢܐ: ܘܡܫܕܪ

1, 6, 11 P ܐܘܪܝܠܝܢܘܣ 1 ܡܪܝܐ] P < 2 ܐܝܟ] P ܐܝܟܢܐ ܐܚܕܬ] P + ܡܪܝܐ ܒܐܝܕܐ] P < 3 P ܕܐܘܦܡܝܐ 4 ܐܦ] P ܘ 5 ܒܢܝܪܐ] P + ܡܢܟ ܕܥܒܕܘܬܐ] P ܕܡܪܕܘܬܐ ܡܪܕܝܬܐ ܘܡܫܝܕܐ] P + ܫܪܝܬ 6 ܕܬܪܕܝܢܐ ܕܚܝܦܐ] P ܕܝܢܐ ܕܢܝܪ (sic) 7–8 ܥܠܘܗ ..... ܗܕܐ] P ܗܕܐ ܟܢܫܬܐ ܪܓܫܬ 8–9 ''ܐܘܠܒܢܘܣ ܐܦܝܣ] P < 10 ܘܟܕ] P ܟܕ 10–11 ܐܦܝܣ ܗܘܐ] P ܐܦܝܣܗ 11 ܐܘܠܒܢܘܣ] P *pr.* ܡܕܝܢܐ ܥܠ ܠܗ] P + ܬܠܬܝܡܐ 12 ܐܪܝܟ] P *pr.* ܕ P ܕܐܠܗܐ 13 ܦܘܩܕܢܐ] P ܡܕܝܢܐ ܡܨܡܪܢܐ] P ܡܨܡܪܢܐ ܘܐܝܟ] P ܘ 14 ܘܡܫܕܪ] P ܘܬܫܕܪ

10

ܗܘܐ ܒܕܝܘܣܩܘܪܘܣ ܐܝܟ ܕܐܡܪܐ ܥܠܘܗܝ ܡܫܡܫܢܐ. ܗܘ
ܕܝܢ ܣܦܪܛܠܛܠܘܣ ܘܥܠ ܐܦܝ ܕܐܝܬ ܗܘܐ ܬܡܢ ܒܪ ܥܡܗ܆
ܬܗܘܪܐ ܒܗ ܒܬܪܡܘܕܬܐ ܗܕܐ ܪܒܬܐ܆ ܕܡܦܩ ܐܠܗܐ
ܒܪܒܘܬܗܘܢ ܕܩܕ̈ܝܫܐ ܚܪ̈ܒܐ ܘܫܪ̈ܝܢܐ. ܘܐܬܕܡܪܘ
ܕܒܡܐ ܐܡܪܝܢ ܠܒܬܘܠܬܐ ܗܘ ܘܠܐ ܐܒ. ⁘. ܗܿܘ ܕܝܢ 43
ܐܣܦܪܛܠܛܠܘܣ ܒܝܒܘܬܐ ܦܘܕ ܘܐܝܬܝܘܗܝ، ܠܗܘ
ܠܒܬܘܠܬܐ ܗܝ ܐܝܟܐ ܕܫܒܝܩ ܗܘܐ ܠܗܘܢ ܘܐܦ ܠܗ
ܠܛܠܝܬܐ ܐܘܦܡܝܐ. ܘܒܪ ܐܬܘ ܐܘܢܡܘ ܐܝܟܢ ܡܕܒܪܘܗܝ،
ܕܐܣܦܪܛܠܛܠܘܣ. ܘܡܕܡ ܒܗܢܐ ܙܗܝܐ ܘܡܕܒܪܢܐ
ܐܘܠܨܢܗܘܢ ܐܦܝܣܩܘܦܐ. ܘܒܥܬ ܥܠܘܗܝ ܡܕܒܪܢܘܬܐ.
ܘܦܩܕܘ ܗܘܘ ܕܢܬܦܪܐ ܡܕܡ ܕܒܬܝܒ ܗܘܐ ܒܗܘ
ܕܕܝܣܩܘܪܘܣ. ܕܢܫܒܩܘܢ ܠܒܬܘܠܬܐ ܘܛܠܝܬܐ. ܘܡܢ ܕܐܬܦܪܝ،
ܥܠܝܗ ܚܐܠܘܗܝ، ܠܒܬܘܠܬܐ ܘܐܡܪܘ ܠܗ. ܫܪܝܪ ܡܕܡ
ܕܫܒܩܬ ܕܟܬܝܒ ܒܕܝܣܩܘܪܘܣ ܗܢܐ. ܗܘ ܕܝܢ ܠܒܬܘܠܬܐ
ܦܢܝ ܕܐܡܪ ܡܢܝ، ܫܪܝܪ ܘܠܝܬ ܒܗ ܡܠܬܐ ܕܠܬܐ ܐܦܠܐ

1 P ܒܕܝܣܩܘܪܘܣ ܥܠܘܗܝ ܡܫܡܫܢܐ] P ~ 2 P ܐܣܦܪܛܠܛܐܠܛܠܘܣ 3 ܬܗܘܪܐ] P ܬܗܪ̣ܐ 4 ܕܩܕ̈ܝܫܐ ܚܪ̈ܒܐ ܘܫܪ̈ܝܢܐ] P ܕܗ̈ܘܕܝܐ ܡܩܕ̈ܫܐ 6 & 9 P ܐܣܦܪܛܐܠܛܠܘܣ ܒܝܒܘܬܐ] P + ܪܒܬܐ ܕܒܬܘܠܬܐ ܗ̇، P ܦܘܕܘ ܐܝܬܝܘܗܝ، (sic) 7 ܐܝܟܐ] P ܐܟܝܢ ܠܗ] P < 8 P ܐܘܦܡܝܐ ܐܘܢܡܘ] P ܐܘܢܝܡ ܡܕܒܪܘܗܝ، ܕ] P ܡܕܡ ܒܫܒܥܝܢܐ 9 ܙܗܝܐ ܘܡܕܒܪܢܐ] P ܕܐܠܗܐ 10 ܐܘܠܨܢܗܘܢ] P ܡܢܝ، ܐܘܠܨܢܗܘܢ 11 P ܘܦܩܕ ܗܘܐ 12 P ܒܕܝܣܩܘܪܘܣ ܗܘ 13 ܠܒܬܘܠܬܐ] P + ܗܘ 14 P ܒܕܝܣܩܘܪܘܣ ܠܒܬܘܠܬܐ] P + ܚܠܒܐ 15 ܦܢܝ] P + ܘܐܡܪ ܦܬܓܡܐ

ܫܠܝܢ̇ ܠܛܠܝܘܬܐ. ܟܕ ܢܦܩܐ ܗܘܐ ܕܠܐ ܫܒܩ ܗܘܐ
ܐܢܬܬܐ ܒܐܬܪܗ. ܘܕܐܝܟܢܐ ܢܦܩ ܘܣܦܩ ܠܗܘܢ ܚܪ̈ܒܐ
ܡܘ̈ܕܝܢܐ ܣܗ̈ܕܐ ܢܨܝ̈ܚܐ. ܘܕܐܝܟܢܐ ܐܘܫܛ ܡܫܝܚܐ
ܘܕܟܪܗ̇ ܡܢ ܟܠܗܘܡܟܐ ܕܣܒܪܬ̇ ܟܪ̈ܣܡܘܢ ܕܣܗ̈ܕܐ
ܘܕܢ̈ܟܐ ܫܡܘܥܢܐ ܘܚܘܪ̈ܐ ܘܢܒܕܒܕ: ܘܕܐܝܟܢܐ ܐܬܢܣܝܘ
ܠܗ̇ ܟܕ ܣܒܝܥܐ ܒܡܟܪܬܐ. ܟܕ ܡܠܝܢ ܒܠܘܗܪܐ ܪ̈ܒܐ
ܘܥܒܘܫܐ. ܘܟܠܠܗ ܪ̈ܘܫܐ ܣܪ̈ܐ ܕܥܠܕܐ. ܟܕ ܦܫ ܡܢܗܘܢ
ܪ̈ܘܫܐ ܒܥܡܕܟܐ ܕܗܘ̈ܪܡܟܐ. ܘܕܐܝܟܢܐ ܐܬܢܣܝܘܗ̇ ܒܠܠܝܐ
ܚܕ ܡ̈ܫܡܘܕܝܐ ܦ̈ܠܚܝܐ ܀ ܘܢܒܝܬܘ ܗܘܘ ܘܐܘܕܝܢܘܗܝ
ܠܟܗܢܐ ܢܦܫܐ ܘܡܪܝܐ ܐܘܠܘܓܝܣ ܐܦܝܣܩܘܦܐ.
ܘܡܗܒܠ ܠܗ ܕܢܫܘܠܝܢ ܗ̇ܘ. ܗ̇ܘ ܕܝܢ ܒܗܢܐ. ܟܕ ܐܬܡܢܝ،
ܡܕܡܟܗܘܢ، ܗ̇ܘ ܡܕܡ ܕܐܬܟܬܒ. ܬܒܗ ܗܘܐ ܐܦ ܐܬܕܡܪ
ܒܡܪܝܘܬܗ ܕܠܒܪܐ ܗ̇ܘ. ܘܐܬܬܘܝ ܒܗ̇ ܠܒܝܢܐ 42
ܦܠܣܐ. ܐܦ ܐܬܟܠܠ ܠܗ ܟܠ ܣܘܟܪܢܐ ܗܢܐ. ܘܟܢ
ܗܘܐ ܡܠܝܪܘܣ ܕܠܘܗ ܟܡ ܡܕܝܢܐ ܗ̇ܘ ܦܪܘܟܝܪܐ ܕܒܢܬ
ܣܗ̈ܕܐ ܡܕ̈ܝܢܐ ܡܘ̈ܕܝܢܐ. ܘܠܘܬ ܡܥܒܕܢܐ ܐܣܦܪܛܠܛܝܣ
ܐܘܠ ܘܐܘܕܝܒܗ. ܟܕ ܐܬܡܢܝ، ܡܕܡܟܗܘܢ، ܗ̇ܘ ܡܕܡ ܕܒܬܒ.

3 ܡܫܝܚܐ] P ܐܝܕܗ 4 ܕܣܗ̈ܕܐ] P < ܣܗ̈ܕܐ
6 ܟܕ .... ܒܡܟܪܬܐ] P ܟܠܗ ܡܟܪܬܐ ܪ̈ܒܐ] P ܟܒܝܪܐ
7 ܘܥܒܘܫܐ] P ܘܥܒܘܫܝܐ ܘܟܠܠܗ] P ܘܟܠܠ ܟܕ ܦܫ]
P ܘܦܫ 8 ܒܥܡܕܟܐ] P < P ܒܠܠܝܐ ܚܕ 9 ܘܢܒܝܬܘ]
P ܘܐܬܘ 10 ܐܘܠܘܓܝܣ] P ܐܘܠܘܓܝܘܣ ،ܡܪܝ 11 P
ܕܐܠܗܐ + ܒܗܢܐ] P ܗ̇ܘ ܗ̇ܘ] P ܕܣܘܡܐܠܝܘ
12 ܐܦ] P ܘ 14 ܐܦ] P ܘ 15 ܡܠܝܪܘܣ] P pr. ܠ
ܕܠܘܗ] P + ܠܘܗ 17 ܐܘܠ] P ܘܐܘܠܘ (sic) ܘܐܘܕܝܒܗ]
P ܘܐܘܕܝܒܗ، ܟܕ] P ܘܟܕ

ܘܐܘܕܥܬܗ̇ ܡܪܕܘܬܗ، ܟܕ ܐܡܪܐ ܠܗ. ܡܪܝ ܐܢܬ ܠܗ̇
ܠܛܠܝܬܐ ܗܕܐ ܒܕܘܟ: ܡܪܝ ܐܢܬ ܐܡܪܐ ܚܒܝܒܘܬܗ̇.
ܕܪ̈ܟܐ ܗ̇ܢܘܢ ܕܝܗܒܬ ܠܝ ܗ̇ܢܘܢ ܐܝܬܝܗܘ̇ ܠܝ. ܢܝ̈ܫܐ
ܕ̈ܘܟܝܐ ܡܠܦ̈ܢܘܬܗ، ܕܐܬܪ̈ܝܢ: ܗ̇ܢܘܢ ܦܢܘܗ̇ ܡܢ
ܥܘܠ ܬܘܬܝܬܐ. ܗ̈ܘܕܐ ܗܠܝܢ ܡܕܘ̈ܟܐ ܕܐܒܫܠܬ
ܘܡܒܝܢ ܢܒܠܬܐ ܘܕܒܪܬܗ̇ ܡܒܢܘܢ. ܗ̇ܢܘܢ ܫܘܒܚܗ̇
ܡܢ ܡܒܢܐ ܕܟܠ ܚܒܝܒܘܬܗ̇ ܒܢܝ̈ܗ̇. ܠܦܪܐ ܘܫܘܒܚܐ
ܘܫܒܝܚ. ܗܘܘ ܠܗ̇ ܕܒ̈ܘܒܐ ܩܠܝܠܬܐ ܘܦܠܛܘܗ̇ ܡܢ
41 ܐܪ̈ܕܘܒܢ. ܀ ܗ̇ܘ ܕܝܢ ܟܕ ܫܡܥܬ ܗܠܝܢ: ܘܚܙܐ ܐܦ
ܠܛܠܝܬܐ ܐܫܬܘܠܦ ܠܒܢܐ ܕܐܦ̈ܘܗܝ. ܘܐܝܟ ܡܒܥܬܐ
ܗܒܝܐ ܗ̇ܘܐ ܘܐܫܬܬܩ ܘܠܐ ܐܫܟܚ ܕܢܦܬܚ ܦܘܡܗ:
ܘܢܦܠܐ ܦܬܟܪ̈ܐ ܡܕܡ ܡܢ ܒܗܬܬܐ: ܘܡܢ ܕܚܠܬܐ
ܘܐܘܕܥܬܐ ܕܬܓܠ ܠܟܠܗ̇، ܘܟܠܗܘܢ ܐܝܠܝܢ ܕܐܝܬ ܗܘܘ
ܬܡܢ ܠܟܠܗܘܢ، ܠܛܘܒܬܐ ܗ̇ܘ: ܟܕ ܚܒܫܘܗ̇، ܒܒܝܬܐ
ܟܠܗ ܒܢܬܐ ܘܢܛܪܝܢ ܗܘܘ ܠܗ ܟܠܗܘܢ. ܘܟܕ ܒܕܪܘ
ܕܐܣܛܠܝܢ ܕܥܘܒܕܢܐ ܟܠܗ: ܐܝܟ ܕܗܘܐ ܡܢ ܫܘܪܝܐ
ܘܟܕܡܐ ܠܫܘܠܡܐ: ܘܕܐܝܟܢܐ ܒܡܫ̈ܡܫܬܐ ܗܠܝܢ
ܦܠ̈ܚܬܐ: ܘܟܫܘ̈ܪܝܐ ܙܘ̈ܟܝܐ: ܘܒܬܟܒܐ ܕܦܪܢܣܬܐ

1 & 2 P ܡܪܟܬ   4 P ܡܠܦ̈ܢܝܐ   ܦܢܘܗ̇] P + ܠܝ
5 ܗܠܝܢ ܗ̈ܘܕܐ] P ~   6 ܘܡܒܝܢ] P ܐܝܕܝܢ
10–11 ܗ̇ܘܐ .... ܘܐܝܟ] P ܡܒܥܬܐ ܐܝܟ ܘܗ̇ܘܐ   12 P
ܦܬܟܪܐ   P ܒܗܬܬܗ   P ܕܚܠܬܗ   13 ܕܬܓܠ]
P ܕܢܓܠܬ   14 ܠܛܘܒܬܐ ܗ̇ܘ] P ܠܒܪܐ ܗ̇ܘ ܠܛܘܒܬܐ
ܟܕ] P ܘ   15 ܘܢܛܪܝܢ] P ܟܕ ܢܛܪܝܢ   16 ܕܐܣܛܠܝܢ]
P ܕܐܣܛܐܠܝܢ   17 ܗܠܝܢ] P <

38 ܡܬܠܒܒܘܢ ܡܛܠ ܢܘܟܪܝܘܬܗ ܕܐܘܪܚܐ ܀ ܗܘ ܕܝܢ ܢܟܠܐ
ܦܬܚ ܦܘܡܗ ܕܓܠܐܝܬ ܘܐܡܪ ܠܗ̇: ܕܒܫܘܠܡܢܐ ܐܙܠܝܢ
ܒܫܠܡܐ ܒܟܠܗ̇ ܐܘܪܚܐ. ܘܡܛܝܢ ܠܡܕܝܢܬܢ ܒܚܕܘܐ
ܘܒܫܝܢܘܬܐ. ܘܠܝܬ ܠܝ ܦܠܐ ܒܢܝܐ ܘܫܠܡܢܝܢ. ܘܒܪܬܗ̇
ܫܪܟܐ ܫܠܡܝܢ. ܘܦܓܪܝ ܦܠܚܐ ܠܟܝ. ܘܢܟܝܢܐ ܡܕܡ
ܠܝܬ ܠܗ̇. ܘܐܬܝܠܕ ܠܝ ܒܪܐ ܕܒܪܐ. ܘܟܠ ܕܪܚܡܬܝ،
ܟܢܫܘܢ ܐܝܬܘܗܝ ܢܣܒܘܢ. ܘܐܠܘ ܠܐ ܕܡܣܬܪܗܒܐܝܬ
ܢܦܩܢ ܡܢ ܐܬܪܢ. ܒܗܢܐ ܡܬܠܒܒܢܐ ܗܘܝܬ ܕܐܬܐܬܐ
39 ܬܫܥܝܬ. ܘܟܕ ܫܡܥܬ ܗܘܦܡܝܐ ܡ̈ܠܐ ܗܠܝܢ ܕܕܓܠܘܬܐ
ܡܢ ܗܘ ܓܒܪܐ. ܐܬܬܙܝܥܬ ܘܪܬܬ ܢܦܫܗ̇ ܘܐܙܕܥܙܥܬ
ܒܩܠܐ ܪܡܐ ܘܐܡܪܬ. ܡܢܐ ܥܒܕ ܠܒܪܬܝ ܢܟܠܐ
ܘܕܓܠܐ. ܗܠܝܢ ܐܝܟ ܡܘܬܪܢܝ: ܗܘ ܦܘܩܕܢܐ ܕܐܦܩܕܬ
ܠܝ. ܒܪ̈ܬܐ ܕܦܩܕܬ ܠܝ ܦܝܣܘܢ ܡܬܠܒܒܝܢ ܫܢܝ ܢܟܠܐ. ܀
40 ܘܟܕ ܗܠܝܢ ܐܡܪܬ: ܐܦܩܬܗ̇ ܠܒܪܬܗ̇ ܐܘܦܡܝܐ

1 ܡܛܠ ܢܘܟܪܝܘܬܗ ܕܐܘܪܚܐ.] P ܒܗ̇، ܕܡܕܒܪܐ ܗܘܝܬ
ܠܗ̇ ܠܒܪܬܝ، ܘܐܡܪܝܢ ܢܦܩܘܢ ܡܟܐ. ܘܡܠܗܕܐ ܪܒܢܐ
ܗܘܝܬ. ܡܛܠ ܕܒܐܘܪܚܐ ܢܘܟܪܝܬܐ ܐܝܬ ܗܘܐ ܠܟܘܢ
ܕܬܐܙܠܘܢ. ܕܠܐ ܢܦܩܐ ܠܗ̇ ܗܘܐ ܠܒܪܬܝ، ܡܢ ܚܫܘܫܐ
ܕܐܘܪܚܐ. 3 ܒܫܠܡܐ] P pr. ܘ ܠܡܕܝܢܬܢ] P ܠܐܬܪܢ
5 ܫܠܡܝܢ] P + ܦܨܝ ܘܢܟܝܢܐ ܡܕܡ] P ܘܡܕܡ ܢܟܝܢܐ
6 ܕܪܚܡܬܝ، P] L ܕܪܚܡܬ 7 ܢܣܒܘܢ] P ܢܣܒܐ
8 ܡܬܠܒܒܢܐ . . . . ܕܐܬܐܬܐ] P ܐܬܝܐ ܗܘܬ ܠܡܗܪܒܐ
9 ܬܫܥܝܬ] P pr. ܕ 10 P ܘܗ̇ ܓܒܪܐ ܘܐܙܕܥܙܥܬ]
P ܘܐܬܬܪܗܒܬ ܘܐܬܠܠܬ 11 ܥܒܕ] P ܥܒܕܬ 11, 12 ܢܟܠܐ
ܘܕܓܠܐ] P < 12, 13 P ܕܠܐ ܐܘܒܕܬ 14 P ܐܘܦܡܝܐ

ܟܕ ܐܡܪܝܢ ܠܗ. ܕܒܒܝܫܬܐ ܕܫܡܥܬܟ ܦܠܐ ܗܘܐ ܕܬܬܪܐ
ܘܬܬܒܝܫ. ܘܠܬܬܡ ܘܕܡ ܗܘܐ ܕܐܘܠܬ ܬܘܪܓܐܝܬ. ܡܛܠ
ܕܡܕܪܫܬܐ ܦܠܣܛܝܢܬܐ ܐܝܬܝܗ ܡܬܠܬܠܒܢ: ܘܦܠܓܝ
ܪܥܠܐ ܕܬܫܥܝܬ. ܡܛܠ ܒܪܬܗ. ܘܟܕ ܬܪܠܬ ܐܘܣܒܝܘܣ
ܠܟܬܒܘܗܝ ܕܦܘܩܢܐ ܫܡܥܬܗ. ܗܝ ܕܝܢ ܐܝܬܬܐ ܡܗܝܡܢܬܐ 37
ܦܘܩܢܐ: ܢܦܫܬܗ ܗܘܬ ܠܐܘܦܡܢܐ ܒܪܬܗ ܒܡܦܠܘܬܐ.
ܕܠܐ ܬܬܒܝܫܐ ܗܘܬ ܠܗ ܕܫܡܥܬܐ. ܐܝܟ ܕܟܕ ܕܬܬܦܪܫܐ
ܟܠܗ ܕܚܠܬܗ ܘܟܠܝܗ ܕܡܚܪ ܐܝܕܝܥܗܝܢ ❖ ܘܟܕ ܐܬܒܢܝܘ
ܠܗܘܢ ܡܟܬܒܢܐ ܘܟܬܒܐ ܒܥܝܢ ܟܠܗܝ، ܕܒܥܪܐ ܒܛܘܗ
ܕܒܬܗ. ܢܕܪܬ ܦܘܩܢܐ ܫܡܥܬܗ ܕܬܫܐܠܝܗ ܠܒܝܬܐ ܟܕ
ܐܡܪܬ. ܕܝܢ ܦܠܝܢ ܒܪܝ ܘܕܝܢ ܦܠܢ ܕܐܘܦܡܢܐ ܒܪܬܗ.
ܕܝܢ ܒܒܝܬܗ ܒܟܘܢ ܐܘܪܚܐ. ܐܬܬܠܕ ܠܟܘܢ ܒܪܝ. ܕܟܪܐ
ܗܘ ܐܘ ܢܩܒܬܐ. ܦܠܓܐ ܓܝܪ ܒܡܪܝܬܐ ܐܢܬ، ܗܘܝܬ

1 ܕܒܒܝܫܬܐ] P ܒܒܝܫܬܗ   ܗܘܐ] P + ܠܟ   2 ܘܬܬܒܝܫ
ܘܬܬܪܐܝܟ ܡܛܠܬܗ P ܡܛܠ ܒܪܬܗ]   4 < P]...ܕܐܘܠܬ
ܘܟܕ ܬܪܠܬ] P ܘܟܕ ܫܡܥ ܠܗ ܦܘܩܢܐ ܫܡܥܬܗ. ܘܬܪܠܬ
ܐܝܬܬܐ] P ܕܐܘܦܡܢܐ   5 ܕܦܘܩܢܐ ܫܡܥܬܗ] P ܘܬܪܠܬ
ܒܡܦܠܘܬܐ] P ܠܒܪܬܗ   6 ܠܐܘܦܡܢܐ ܒܪܬܗ] P <
ܠܫܡܥܬܐ] P ܠܗ]   7 ܕܠܐ] P pr. ܐܝܟ   P + ܢܕ
ܐܬܒܢܝܘ] (sic) ܐܝܕܝܥܗܝܢ P 8   ܘܡܚܪ P ܐܝܟ ܕܟܕ]
ܠܗܘܢ] P + ܒܛܘܗ]   ܡܟܬܒܢܐ P 9   ܒܥܝܢ P
ܠܒܝܬܐ] P <   ܘ .pr P]ܢܕܪܬ 10   ܠܟ P]ܟܠܗܝ، ܕ
< P]ܒܪܝ   ܕܐܬܬ P]ܕܝܢ   ܠܗ + P]ܐܡܪܬ 11
(sic) ܢܩܒܬܐ P   < P]ܗܘ 13   ܕܐܘܦܡܢܐ P

ܘܪ̈ܚܡܐ. ܐܝܟ ܗܘ ܒܡܫܠܡܘܬ ܕܠܐ ܚܣܝܪܗ ܘܠܐ ܐܫܬܘܕܥܗ: ܒܟܪ ܡܢܗ ܪܘܚܐܝܬ ܘܠܐ ܐܬܦܠܓ ܒܠܘܬܗ̇ ܘܠܐ ܡܛܠ ܒܢܝܗ. ܐܠܐ ܫܠܛܗ ܐܝܟ ܠܐ ܥ̇ܒܕ ܠܗ. ܘܒܗ̇ ܒܫܒܬܐ ܬܪܝܨܐܝܬ ܠܬ̈ܠܝܬܝܗܘܢ ܕܩܢܘ̈ܡܐ ܘܕܐܘܣܝܐ ܫܠܡ ܗܘܐ ܠܒܪܐ ܗܘ ܫܒܝܚܘܬܗܘܢ. ܕܢܘܗܪ. ܐܝܟ ܡܛܠ ܠܒܪܐ ܗܘ ܠܡܠܬܐ ܘܐܡܪ ܗܘܐ ܠܗܘܢ. ܕܗܘ ܢܒܠܐ ܘܪ̈ܚܡܐ ܕܚܝܐ ܢܬܕܥܘܢ ܒܠܗ ܗܘ ܢܒܠܐ ܘܒܪܫܬܐ ܪ̈ܚܡܬܐ. ܘܡܫܟܚܐ ܚܝܠܘܬܗ ܘܡܛܠܠ ܒܢܝܗ. ܐܠܐ ܐܬܦܪ̈ܫܘ ܠܗ ܘܫܪܝܢ ܐܝܟܢܐ ܦܠܐ ܕܢܫܬܒܪ ܫܘܒܪܢܐ ܗܢܐ ܀ ܗ̇ܢܘܢ ܕܝܢ. ܡܫܡܗܐ ܒܢ̈ܝܢ ܫܪ̈ܒܝܬܗܘܢ ܘܒ̈ܢܝ ܠܒܢܝ̈ܢܗܘܢ ܒܠܚܘܕ. ܘܗܕܐ ܐܬܦܫܩܘ ܗܘܘ. ܕܠܐ ܐܢܫ ܢܦܠܐ ܠܗ ܕܐܬܪܬܗ̇، ܠܗ̇ ܒܪܬܗ ܐܘܣܝܐ ܠܐܬܪܐ ܗܢܐ. ܘܢܩܘܡ ܠܡܒܢܝܗ ܠܒܝܬܐ ܗܘ ܒܠܗ ܒܪܘܚܗ̇ ܒܫܠܛܢܐ. ܘܟܕ ܐܫܟܚܘܗ̇ ܡܛܠܘ ܒܢܝܗ ܒܫܘܟܢܐ

1 ܟܕܪ . . . ܪܘܚܐܝܬ] P < 3 ܘܠܐ ܡܛܠ ܒܢܝܗ] P ܘܡܛܠ ܒܢܝܗ ܕܠܒܪܐ ܗܘ ܐܒܝܐ ܕܦܠܐ ܗܘܐ ܠܗ ܥܠ ܘܡܛܠ ܒܢܝܗ 3–4 ܫܠܛܗ . . . ܠܗ] P ܕܢܛܠܠ ܠܬܠܝܬܝܗܘܢ 4 Pcorr ܪܘܚܐܝܬ. ܘܠܐ ܐܬܦܠܓ ܒܠܘܬܗ̇ 5 P ܘܕܐܘܣܝܐ P ܫܒܝܚܘܬܗܘܢ 6 ܕܢܘܗܪ . . . ܠܡܠܬܐ] P ܕܢܘܗܪ ܗܘܐ ܠܗ ܠܡܠܬܐ ܗܘ 7 P ܢܬܕܥܘܢ 7–8 ܒܠܗ . . . . ܘܒܪܫܬܐ] P ܗܕܐ ܒܠܗ̇ ܒܪܫܬܐ 9 P ܘܒ̈ܢܝ ܠܒܢܝܢܗܘܢ 10 ܗ̇ܢܘܢ] P ܗ̇ܢܝܢ ܫܪ̈ܒܝܬܗܘܢ 11 P ܘܒ̈ܢܝ ܠܒܢܝܢܗܘܢ 12 ܠܗ] P + ܠܡܠܬܐ ܗܘ ܕܐܬܪܬܗ̇، ܠܗ̇ ܒܪܬܗ] P ܕܐܬܪܬܐ ܒܪܬܗ 13 P ܘܫܠܛ ܠܒܢܝܢܐ ܐܘܣܝܐ P ܦܠܓܘܬܐ ܗܘܐ ܠܒܝܬܗ ܒܠܗ ܠܡܒܢܝܗ ܠܡܠܬܐ ܗܘ

ܒܦܘܪܩܢܐ ܗܢܝܢ. ܐܝܟ ܠܐܠܗܐ ܗܘ ܕܠܐ ܡܬܒܝܢܗ
ܠܐܒܘܗܝ. ܬܘܒ ܕܝܢ ܥܡ ܐܦܘܠܝܢܪܝܘܣ ܚܕ ܕܐܫܬܪܪ ܗܘܐ
ܡܢ ܟܠܒܐ ܠܐܬܪܐ ܗܢܝܢ. ܕܢܦܩܘ ܗܘܐ ܡܢ ܒܥܠܕܒܒܐ.
ܦܪ̈ܫܐ ܒܝܬ ܘܡܘ̈ܬܢܐ. ܕܐܫܬܘܝܘ ܕܢܟܒܕܘܢ ܦܪܟܐ
ܒܐܬܪܐ ܗܢܐ. ܘܐܚܪܢܐ ܕܐܬܬܩܝܡ ܗܘܐ ܦܪܟܘܢ
ܒܝܬܐ ܕܗܘܦ. ܗܟܢܐ ܐܦ ܗܢܐ ܠܟܢܘܫܝܐ ܐܬܬܚܝܕ
ܒܦܘܫܐ ܕܠܒܪ. ܘܐܗܦܟܘܢ ܠܗ ܡܪܐ ܦܘܪܥܢܗ ܒܪܫܗ.
ܘܠܗܘܡܢܐ ܕܢܦܪ ܒܗ ܢܓܠ. ܘܟܡܝܢܘܬܐ ܕܠܒܪ ܐܬܬܚܝܕ:
ܕܢܦܠ ܒܡܘܬܬܐ ܘܟܦܪ ܠܗ ܟܪܘܒܘܬܐ ܕܫܘܕܐ ܩܕܝܫܐ.
ܘܠܐ ܐܦ ܡܢ ܕܢܦܫ ܕܫܠܡܐ ܕܐܠܗܐ. ܘܗܘ ܕܒܐܝܬܘܬܐ 36
ܠܪܠܬܗ. ܕܒܗ ܒܐܬܪܐ ܕܢܦܠ ܡܘܬܬܐ ܘܟܦܠ.
ܡܫܡܫ ܒܪܫܐ ܕܬܒܥܬܐ ܕܢܒܠܗ ܢܦܠ. ⁘ ⁘. ܘܒܚܕ ܡܢ
ܝܘ̈ܡܝܢ: ܟܕ ܗܘ ܠܟܢܘܫܝܐ ܡܫܠܡܝܢ ܒܫܘܒܚܐ. ܚܙܝܗ
ܠܟܪܐ ܚܕ ܫܒܒܘܗܝ ܘܥܠܠ ܒܝܬܗ. ܘܗܘ ܒܥܠܐ

1 ܗܘ ܠܟܢܘܫܝܐ] P ܠܟܢܘܫܝܐ ܗܘ   2 ܬܘܒ] P <
P ܐܦܘܠܝܢܪܝܐܠܠܝܘܣ   4 ܒܝܬ] P <   ܕܐܫܬܘܝܘ]
P ܘܗܘܘ ܕܐܫܬܪܪܘ   5 ܘܐܚܪܢܐ] P ܘܐܚܪܢܝܢ   ܗܘܐ]
P <   6 ܗܢܐ ܠܟܢܘܫܝܐ] P ܗܘ ܠܟܢܘܫܝܐ   7 ܒܦܘܫܐ]
P *pr.* ܒܗ   ܠܗ] P <   ܦܘܪܥܢܗ] P ܚܘܠܗ   9 P
ܘܟܐܦܪ   P ܟܪܘܒܘܬܗܘܢ   10 ܐܦ ... ܕܐܠܗܐ]
P ܐܦ ܠܒܗ   10—11 ܘܗܘ .... ܠܪܠܬܗ] P ܘܠܪܠܬܗ
ܗܘ ܕܒܐܝܬܘܬܐ   11 ܕܒܗ] P < ܒܗ   12 ܡܫܡܫ] P *pr.*
ܒܗ ܢܦܠ   P ܘܬܒܥܬܐ   ܢܦܠ] P <   13 ܘܗܘ
ܡܫܠܡܝܢ ܒܫܘܒܚܐ ܗܘ ܠܟܢܘܫܝܐ ܒܥܠܐ] P ....ܒܫܘܒܚܐ
14 ܫܒܒܘܗܝ] P ܡܢ ܫܒ̈ܒܘܗܝ   14—1 ...ܘܗܘ
ܒܝܬܗ] P ܫܒ̈ܒܐ ܠܟܢܘܫܝܐ ܗܘܐ ܕܗܘܝ ܚܕ ܗܢܐ

ܕܝܢ ܐܡܪܗ̇ ܘܐܬܢܛܪܬ ܠܗ̇ ܣ̈ܓܝܐܐ ܕܬܠܡܕ. ܘܢܬ̈ܟܢܫܘܢ ܬܡܢ ܝܘܡܢܐ ܗܘ̇ ܟܠܗ ܀ ܒܬܪ ܕܝܢ ܙܒ̇ܢ ܗܘܐ ܫܡܥܐ ܠܡܕܝܢܬ. ܢܫ̈ܬܘܢ ܠܬܠܡ̈ܝܕܘܗܝ ܕܗ̇ ܕܡܘܕܝܢ ܠܐܠܗܐ ܟܠ ܣܘܓܐܐ ܕܫܠ̈ܝܚܘܬܗ ܕܫܡܥܘ ܡܐܕܝܘܢ. ܘܠܒܬܪܗ ܕܝܢ ܕܝܘܡܢܐ ܢܦܩ ܗܘܐ ܠܓܒܐ ܕܗܢܐ ܫܘܒܚܐ ܒܟܠܗ̇ ܡܕܝܢܬܐ. ܘܐܬܒܢܝܬ ܒܝܫܘܗ̇ ܘܒ̈ܢܝ ܥܡܡܘܬܗ̇. ܘܒܬܪ ܚܐܘܗ̇ ܚܙܝܗ. ܘܐܘܕܝܘ ܠܐܠܗܐ ܗܘ̇ ܕܠܐ ܡܗܝܡܢܐ ܡܢ ܦܘܠܚܢܗܘܢ. ܘܒܬܪ ܢܬ̈ܩܢ ܗ̈ܘܘ ܐܒܝܕܐ. ܐܡܝܢ ܗ̈ܘܘ ܒܝܠܘܬܐ ܒܒܝܬܗ ܕܐܠܗܐ. ܒܝܘܡܐ ܕܝܢ ܕܚܕܒܫܒܐ ܘܕܥܪܘܒܬܐ: ܨܠܝܢ ܗ̈ܘܘ ܒܟܠܝܢ ܘܬܪ̈ܝܢ ܝܘܡܐ ܟܠܗ ܡܕܡ ܠܘܩܒܠܐ ܕܫܘܪܝܐ ܡܬܝܩܢ ܒܟܠܗ̇ ܢܦܘܫܬܐ .܀.

35 ܘܡܢ ܒܬܪ ܩܠܝܠ ܙܒܢܐ: ܗܘ̇ ܚܝܠܐ ܬܘܩܦܐ ܕܒܢܘܢ: ܕܠܐ ܡܬܬܡܠܠ ܘܠܐ ܡܬܦܫܩ. ܚܘܝ ܬܘܒܬܗ ܐܝܟ ܕܩܒܠ. ܘܒܐܝܢܐ ܐܬܬܚܝܪܬ ܟܠ ܚܘܠܐ ܘܕܪܟܐ ܒܘܬܐ ܗܘ. ܘܒܬܪ ܡܕܒܪܢܘܬܐ ܕܐܠܗܐ ܕܗܘܬ

1 ܘܐܬܢܛܪܬ] P ܘܐܬܢܛܪܘ ܘܢܬ̈ܟܢܫܘܢ] P ܘܢܬܟܢܫܘ 2 ܟܠܗ] P < ܒܬܪ ܕܝܢ] P ܡܢ ܕܝܢ ܕ ܗܘܐ] P < ܫܡܥܐ] P ܝܘܡܢܐ 3 ܢܫ̈ܬܘܢ] P ܢܫ̈ܬܘ ܠܬܠܡ̈ܝܕܘܗܝ L* 4 P ܡܐܕܝܘܢ 4–5 ܘܠܒܬܪܗ ܕܝܢ ܕܝܘܡܢܐ] P ܘܒܬܪܗ ܕܝܘܡܢܐ ܗܘ̇ 5 P ܠܓܒܐ 6 P ܘܐܬܒܢܝܘ ܥܡܡܘܬܗ̇] P + ܟܠܗܘܢ 7 P ܚܐܘܗ̇ ܗܘ̇] P < 8 ܘܒܬܪ] P ܒܬܪ ܐܒܝܕܐ] P < ܐܡܝܢ ܗ̈ܘܘ] P ܘܐܡ̈ܝܢܝܢ 9–10 ܘܬ̈ܪܝܢ ... ܝܘܡܐ] P ܘܒܥܪܘܒܬܐ ܘܒܥܝܢ ܒܥܒܐ. ܠܐ ܬܡܠܝܢ ܗ̈ܘܘ ܡܢ ܕܨܠܝܢ ܗ̈ܘܘ ܘܬܪ̈ܝܢ 10 ܝܘܡܐ ܟܠܗ] P ~ 12 ܕܒܢܘܢ] P ܕܒܗܘܢ 15 ܘܒܬܪ] P < ܒܬܪ

ܚܕܬܗ̇ ܠܒܪܬܗ̇ ܘܠܐ ܐܫܬܘܕܥܬܗ̇: ܒܗ̇ܝ ܕܠܒܝܫܐ
ܗܘܬ ܡܫ̈ܟܢܐ ܕܡܘܟܟܐ. ܒܪܬܗ̇ ܕܝܢ ܐܫܬܘܕܥܬܗ̇
ܠܐܡܗ̇: ܘܡܪܒܝܬ ܘܣܓܕܬ ܠܗ̇ ⁘ ܟܕ ܕܝܢ ܐܫܬܘܕܥܬ
ܐܡܗ̇ ܕܒܪܬܗ̇ ܗܝ: ܪܘܚ ܢܒܝܘܬܐ ܕܬܪ̈ܬܝܗܝܢ. ܡܢ
ܣܦܪܐ ܘܢ̈ܡܘܣܐ. ܘܡ̈ܫܒܚܢ ܗ̈ܘܘ, ܚܕܐ ܠܚܕܐ. ܘܠܐ
ܡ̈ܫܬܒܩܢ ܗ̈ܘܘ, ܕܢܡ̈ܠܠܢ ܥܡ ܚ̈ܕܕܐ ܡܢ ܟܒܝܐ ܣܓܝܐܐ ⁘

34 ܘܟܕ ܒܕܢܐ ܣܓܝܐܐ ܗ̈ܘܘ: ܒܢܝܘ ܐܢ̈ܫܐ ܕܒܢܬ ܣܗ̈ܕܐ.
ܘܟܠ ܡ̈ܢ ܕܐܫܬܟܚ ܬܡܢ ܒܢܬ ܣܗ̈ܕܐ ܬܡܗܝܢ ܗܘܐ
ܥܠ ܟܒܝܐ ܕܐܝܟܢܐ ܗܘܐ ܠܬܪ̈ܬܝܗܝܢ. ܩܕܝܡ ܫܐܠܗ̇
ܗܘܐ ܗܘ̇ ܦܪܘܣܢܝܐ ܠܐܘܦܘܡܝܐ. ܕܬܬܢܐ ܡܕܡ ܐܡܗ̇
ܡܕܡ ܕܬܕܥ ܡܢܗܘܢ. ܘܬܚܘܐ ܡܕܡ ܐܡܗ̇ ܘܡܕܡ ܐܚܪܝܢ
ܕܐܫܬܘܕܥܬ ܠܗ ܡܕܡ ܕܥܒܕ ܠܗ̇ܬܗ̇: ܫܠܐ ܐܠܗܐ ܕܢܝܪܐ
ܠܡܪ̈ܡܝܗܘܢ ܕܣܗ̈ܕܐ ܦܪ̈ܝܫܐ ܡܘܕ̈ܝܢܐ. ܘܕܐܝܟܢ
ܐܦܘܗ̇ ܡܕ̈ܝܢܬܐ ܡܢ ܡܕܝܢܬܐ ܕܢܦܩܬܐ ܗܘܬ ܒܗ:
ܘܐܝܬܝܗ̇ ܒܠܠܐ ܕܡܫܘܚܬܐ ܣܓܝܐܐ. ܘܟܠ ܡܢ ܕܫܡܥ
ܐܡܪ, ܘܫܒܚ ܠܐܠܗܐ ܕܥܒܕ ܛܝܒܘܬܐ ܕܪ̈ܚܡܘܗܝ. ܕܪܒܬ

2 ܕܡܘܟܟܐ] P ܡ̈ܟܟܐ   3 P ܘܣܓܕܬ   4 ܐܡܗ̇ LP*]
ܠܒܪܬܗ̇: ܘܡܪܒܝܬ ܕܒܪܬܗ̇ P [ܕܒܪܬܗ̇ ܗ̇ܝ,   ܐܡܗܐ Pcorr
[ܚܕܐ ܠܚܕܐ   P ܕܢ̈ܡܘܣܐ [ܘܢ̈ܡܘܣܐ 5   ܗ̇ܝ, ܐܝܬܝܗ̇
ܚܕܐ ܥܡ ܚܕܐ P [ܥܡ ܚ̈ܕܕܐ 6   P ܠܚ̈ܕܕܐ
8 ܬܡܗܝܢ] P ܬܡܗܝܢ   9 ܕܐܝܟܢܐ ܗܘܐ ܠ] P ܕ   [ܗܘܝܢ P
L ܕܝܢ ܗ̈ܘ (sic)   10 ܗܘ̇] P <   P ܠܐܘܦܘܡܝܐ
10–12 ܡܕܡ ܐܡܗ̇... ܡܕܡ] P ܒܠܚܘܕ   13 [ܠܡܪ̈ܡܝܗܘܢ
P ܥܠ ܡܪ̈ܡܝܗܘܢ   [ܡܘܕ̈ܝܢܐ] P <   14 [ܡܕ̈ܝܢܬܐ] P <
16 [ܕܪ̈ܚܡܘܗܝ] P ܠܪ̈ܚܡܘܗܝ

ܘܗܫܐ ܒܡܕܝܢܬܐ ܡܒܪܟܬܐ ܐܘܪܗܝ. ܒܡܫܠܡܐ
ܕܡܫܝܚܐ ܠܥܠܡܝܢ ܒܪ̈ܟܝ ܘܦܘ̈ܡܝ ܘܡܫܒ̈ܚܝܢ ܡܢ ܟ̈ܠܗܘܢ.
ܘܪܝܫܐ ܫܒܝܚܘܬܗܘܢ ܘܫܡܥܝܢ ܚܝܠܐ ܕܝܪܐ ܒܗܘܢ ·܀·܀·
32 ܘܟܕ ܗܠܝܢ ܐܬܓܪܬ ܗܘܬ: ܘܕܡ̈ܥܐ ܬ̈ܢܝܢܘܬܐ ܡܢ ܚ̈ܕܝܝܗ̇
ܥܠ ܠܘܣܡܝܐ ܕܡܕ̈ܝܢܬܐ ܐܫܬܐ ܗܘܬ: ܚܙܐ ܗܘܐ
ܒܗ̇ ܦܘܪܡܢܝܐ ܒܪ ܡܬܕܡܪ. ܘܟܕ ܟ̇ܠܗ ܬܫܡܫܬܐ
ܦܪ̇ܫ ܠܘܬܗ̇ ܘܡܫܐܠ ܗܘܐ ܠܗ̇ ܘܐܡ̇ܪ. ܐܢܬܬܐ
ܡܢܐ ܥܠܝܠܐ ܐܢܬܝ܆ ܘܡܢܐ ܗܘ ܫܘܒܪܝ. ܗ̇ܝ ܕܝܢ
ܡܗܝܡܢܬܐ ܬܪ̈ܬܝ܆ ܘܕܡܘܗ̇ ܥܠܘܗܝ ܫܘܒܪܐ ܕܡܪܝ
33 ܐܠܗܐ ܓܐܕܗ̇. ܡܢ ܫܘܪܝܐ ܘܥܕܡܐ ܠܫܘܠܡܐ ܀ ܘܟܕ
ܗܠܝܢ ܫܡܥ ܦܘܪܡܢܝܐ: ܬܡܗ ܒܪܘܚܗ ܕܫܘܒܪܐ
ܒܕܡܐ ܕܐܦ ܢܬܦܠܓ. ܘܕܢܚܘܩ ܥܠ ܫܪܪܐ ܒܥܐ ܗܘܐ.
ܘܕܢܐܠܦ ܕܪ̈ܬܗ̇ ܕܐܡܗ̇ ܝ̇ܒܐ ܗܘܐ. ܘܒܫܘܠܛܢܐ
ܩܛܝܠܐ ܫܕܪ ܐܢܬ ܗܘܐ ܠܐܡܗ̇: ܕܬܐܠܦ ܗܘܐ
ܡܢܝܢܗ̇: ܕܐ ܐܢܝܢ ܕܐܡܪܬ ܒܪܬܗ̇ ܐܝܬܘܗܝ
ܫܘܒܪܐ ܀ ܟܕ ܕܝܢ ܫܡܥܬ ܐܡܗ̇ ܡܚܕܐ ܐܬܬܗܪܬ
ܥܠܒ. ܒܗ̇ ܕܐܣܒܪܬ ܕܗ̇ܝ ܘܡܠܠܗ̇ ܐܬܐ. ܡܢ ܕܝܢ
ܕܫܠܡܬ ܐܡܗ̇ ܠܒܝܬ ܫܘܕܪܐ ܠܦܘ̈ܠܚܢܐ ܥ̈ܒܕܝܢܐ:

1 ܘܗܫܐ] P + ܡܢ ܦܪܐ 2 P ܘܦܘ̈ܡܝ P ܘܡܫ̈ܒܚܝܢ ܟ̈ܠܗܘܢ] P ܟ̈ܠܗܝܢ 3 ܘܫܡܥܝܢ .... ܒܗܘܢ] P < 4 ܬ̈ܢܝܢܘܬܐ] P ܬܒ̈ܥܬܐ 6 ܡܬܕܡܪ] P ܡܬܕܡܪܪ 7 ܘܐܡ̇ܪ] P < 8 P ܥܠܝܠܬܝ P ܘܡܢܘ 9 P ܬܪ̈ܬܝ ܥܠܘܗܝ ܫܘܒܪܐ] P ܒܥܠܘܗ̇ ܬܕܡܘܪܬܐ 13 P ܕܪܬܐ P ܘܒܫܘܠܛܢܐ 14 P ܫܕܪ ܗܘܐ ܘܐܡܪ 15 ܕܐܡܪܬ] P + ܠܗ 16 ܡܚܕܐ] P < 17 ܕܐܣܒܪܬ] P + ܗܘܬ 18 ܠܦܘ̈ܠܚܢܐ] P *pr.* ܕ

ܗܘܬ. ܘܐܡܝܢ ܕܫܠܡܐ ܢܗܪܐ ܗܘܬ ܠܗ ܠܣܘܒܪܢܐ. ܙܒܢܐ ܗܘܐ ܠܗܘܢ ܒܬܪ ܡܘܡܪܐ ܗܢܐ. ܟܠܗ ܠܘܬ ܐܠܗܐ ܦܢܬ ܘܫܡܫܬܗ̇. ܘܐܬܪܚܡܬ ܟܠܗ ܠܘܬܗ ܘܒܥܘ. ܒܥܘܬܐ ܕܐܘܠܨܢܗ̇ ܠܡܪܢܐ ܫܒܩܬ܀ ܘܝܗܒܐ ܠܗ̇ ܘܦܠܚ ܐܬܠܒܟܬ̇ ܒܦܬܓܡܐ ܗܠܝܢ ܕܬܫܡܫܬܐ ܕܡܫܡܫܝܢ ܗܘܘ. ܘܡܫܒܚܬ̇ ܗܘܬ ܓܝܪ ܠܒܘܣܡܐ ܕܡܕ̈ܢܚܐ ܡ̈ܕܘܢܝܐ. ܘܫܪܬ̇ ܢܦܫܗ̇ ܡܕܡܝܗܘܢ ܘܒܒܥܘܬܐ ܦܠܚܬܐ ܐܡ̈ܪܐ ܗܘܬ. ܥܠ ܕܢܓܕܐ ܡܪܢܐ ܥܒܕ ܒܫܡܝܐ ܘܒܐܪܥܐ. ܕܒܪܫܝܬܐ ܒܒܬܗ̇ ܘܒܦܓܪܐ ܚܕܘܬܐ. ܕܕܝܢ ܡܢ ܫܡܝܐ ܘܦܪܘܩ. ܒܪܝܟ ܐܣܘܪܟ ܡܢ ܐܬܪܟ ܡܪܢܐ. ܕܡܠܝܢ ܫܡܝܐ ܘܐܪܥܐ ܬܫܒ̈ܘܚܬܟ. ܒܪܝܟܐ ܗܘ ܫܒܝܠܬܐ ܕܡܕ̈ܝܢܝܟ. ܒ̇ܪܝܐ ܚܪܒܘܬܗܘܢ ܡܥ̈ܕܝܢܐ ܡܕ̈ܝܢܐ. ܒܪܝܟ ܫܠܝܐ ܕܡܪܘܗܝ. ܗ̇ܘ ܕܒܓ̈ܪܡܘܗܝ ܒܪܐ. ܥܠ ܕܒܗܘܢ ܡܬܚܦܝܢ ܠܐ ܒܥܬ̇. ܥܠ ܕܒܗܘܢ ܢܦܫܢ ܘܠܘܬܗܘܢ ܪܗ̇ܛ. ܠܐ ܫܐܠ. ܫܘܕܝܐ ܠܗܘܢ ܐܡܬܐ ܦܠܚܬܐ ܕܐܬܝ̣ܪܬ. ܡܘܕܝܐ ܠܗܘܢ ܫܒܝܬܐ ܕܐܬܦܢܝܬ ܠܐܬܪܗ̇. ܗܐ ܒܬܪ ܒܪܫܝܬܐ ܥܠ ܪܘܫܡܐ ܦܠܚܬܐ ܐܢܬܝ، ܗܘܝܬ ܒܡܕܝܢܬܐ ܕܠܘܬܢܐ ܓܒܝ.

2 ܒܬܪ] P <   4 P ܘܝܗܒ̣ܝ: *see* p.   ܘܦܠܚ] P <
ܦܠܚ   6 ܗܘܬ] P <   7 P ܘܫܪܬ   8–9 ܥܠ ....
ܘܒܐܪܥܐ] P <   9 ܕܒܪܫܝܬܐ] P < ܕ   10 ܡܪܢܐ] P <
12 ܕܡܕ̈ܝܢܝܟ] P ܕܡܕ̈ܝܢܐ   12–13 ܒܪܝܐ .... ܡܕ̈ܝܢܐ]
P <   13 ܗܘ ܕܒܓ̈ܪܡܘܗܝ] P ܕܒܠ ܒܓ̈ܪܡܘܗܝ
14 ܕܒܗܘܢ] P ܕܠܘܬܗܘܢ   15 ܢܦܫܢ ܘܠܘܬܗܘܢ] P <
17 ܒܬܪ ܒܪܫܝܬܐ] P ∾   18 P ܒܡܕܝܢܬܗ   P ܓܐܒܝ

ܕܐܪ̈ܘܬܐ ܒܒܒܠ܃ ܫܪܘܬܐ ܗܝ ܐܘܪܫܠܡ ܟܕ ܚܒܘܫܘ
ܐܫܬܪܪܬ ܠܗ܃ ܗܟܢܐ ܐܦ ܟܕ ܚܝܠܐ ܐܠܗܝܐ ܕܫܪ̈ܪܐ
ܒܐܪ̈ܡܠܘܬܗܘܢ ܕܣܗ̈ܕܐ ܩ̈ܕܝܫܐ ܘܡܘ̈ܕܝܢܐ܂ ܕܡܪܝ، ܠܗܘܢ
ܘܒܗܘܢ ܐܬܓܠܝܬ܃ ܒܗ ܒܠܠܐ ܐܫܬܒܚܬ ܒܟܠܘܪܐ
ܕܟܠ ܓܒܪ ܒܝܬ ܣܗܕܐ ܡܕܝ̈ܢܐ ܘܡܘ̈ܕܝܢܐ܂ ܘܟܕ ܢܦܩܬ 30
ܡܕܝܢܬܐ ܬܘܗܬ، ܐܝܟ ܕܗܝ ܫܒܝܬܐ܂ ܘܢܦܩܬ، ܠܣܗܕܐ
ܡܕܝܢܐ ܗܕܐ، ܫܡܥܢܐ ܒܟܠܝܘܡܐ ܕܓܒܪܐ ܗܟܢܐ ܕܡܛܐ
ܠܐܕܝܗ ܘܐܡܪ ܠܗ܂ ܡܕܝܢܬܐ ܐܝܟܢܐ، ܕܐܝܟܢܐ ܐܬܬܝܗܒ
ܗܫܐ ܘܐܝܟܢܐ ܦܪܝܟܐ ܐܬܝܗܒ܂ ܗܝ ܕܝܢ ܐܪܝܡܬ ܚ̈ܝܠܝܗ
ܘܢܦܩܬ، ܠܒܝܬܐ ܡܕܝܢܐ ܕܩ̈ܕܝܫܐ܂ ܘܟܕ ܗܘܐ ܗܠܝܢ
ܫܡܝܢܐ܃ ܐܝܠܝܢ، ܕܐܬܒܢܝܬ ܠܒܝܬܐ ܡܕܝܢܐ ܕܣܗ̈ܕܐ܂
ܐܡܪ ܠܗ ܦܠܘܒܐ ܫܡܝܢܐ܂ ܗܘܐ ܓܒܪܐ ܚ̈ܪܝܒܘܬ܂ ܘܠܐ
ܒܥܠܡܐ܂ ܘܒܗ ܒܫܡܝܐ ܐܬܓܠܝ ܣܒܪܗ܂ ܘܢܦܩܬ ܠܒܢܝܢܐ 31
ܘܠܫܡܝܐ ܘܠܟܠ ܕܗܘܐ܂ ܘܠܐ ܬܘܒ ܢܦܬܗ܆ ܘܟܕ ܗܠܝܢ
ܠܬܪܝܢܐ ܕܒܝܬ ܣܗܕܐ܂ ܫܡܝܢܐ ܬܫܡܫܬܐ ܗܝ، ܕܒܢܝܢܐ܂
ܘܐܬܓܠܝܬ ܗܘܬ ܚܕܘܬܐ ܪ̈ܒܬܐ ܘܕܝܠܬܐ ܘܬܫܒܚܬܐ

1 P ܒܒܒܒܠ 2 ܟܕ ܚܝܠܐ] P ܒܚܝܠܐ 3 ܘܡܘܕܝ̈ܢܐ]
P < ܘ ܕܡܪܝ،] P ܕܡܪܟܝ 4 ܘܒܗܘܢ ܐܬܓܠܝܬ]
P < ܒܟܠܘܪܐ] P ܕܐܝܬܝܗ ܒܟܠܘܪܐ ܕܐܘܪܗܝ،
5 ܕܟܠ] P ܟܠ P ܕܡܕܝ̈ܢܐ ܘܡܘ̈ܕܝܢܐ 6 P ܬܘܗܬ
P ܘܢܦܩܬ 7 ܗܕܐ،] P < 8 ܕܐܝܟܢܐ] P < ܕ
10 P ܘܢܦܩܬ 10, 11 P ܦܠܘܒܐ ܫܡܝܢܐ 11 P
ܘܐܡܪܐ ܕܐܬܓܠܝ ܠܒܝܬ ܣܗܕܐ P 13 ܐܬܓܠܝ]
P ܐܬܓܠܝ P ܘܢܦܩܬ 14 ܕܗܘܐ] P ܕܗܘܐ
16 ܗܘܬ] P < ܘܬܫܒܚܬܐ] P ܘܬܫܒܘܚܬܐ (sic)

ܐܠܗܐ ܕܡܠܠ ܫܪܪܐ ܕܡܫܝܚܘܬܟ ܢܫܒܘ ܘܡܕܝܢ̈ܬܟ
ܟܢ̈ܘܫܝܐ ܓܘܪ̈ܝܗܘܢ ܠܡܠܠܐ: ܐܠܗܐ ܕܩܒܠ ܕܒܥ̈ܘܬܗܘܢ
ܕܒܫܢܬܐ ܫܢܬܐ ܘܡܕܡܫܬܟ. ܬܐ ܠܥܘܕܪܢܗ̇ ܕܐܡܬܟ.
ܐܠܗܐ ܕܡܠܠ ܬ̈ܘܠܢܐ ܪܒܢ ܠܒܢܝܐ ܕܝܫܪܝ. ܦܪܘܩܢ
26 ܗܘ ܐܘܠܝܢܐ ܗܢܐ. ܠܩܪܝܢܐ ܘܫܡܘܥܐ ܘܫܟܝܒ:
ܒܢ̈ܘܗܪܐ ܘܡܫܬ̈ܘܬܐ ܕܐܘܪܗ̇ ܡܒܪܟܬܐ. ܒܟܠ ܢܘܪܒܝ
ܒܡܘܪܢܝܗܘܢ. ܒܢ̈ܝ ܟܢ̈ܘܫܝܐ ܡܫܒܚܝܢ ܒܫܒܬܐ ܗܕܐ ܀
27 ܗ̇ܝܕܝܢ ܫܒܚ ܐܠܗܐ ܒܟܠܗ̇ ܬܫܒܘܚܬܗ̇. ܘܡܢ ܫܠ
ܪܘܚܐ ܗ̇ܘ ܫܦܝܪܐ ܘܟܝܢܐ ܕܫܦܝܪܘܬܐ ܕܫܠܝܐ ܗ̇ܝ
ܐܬܗܦܟܬ ܠܪܘܚܐ ܒܫܘܒܚܐ ܕܗܝܡܢܘܬܐ. ܘܒܡܕܒܪܢܘܬܐ
ܕܐܢܫܐ ܬܠܬܐ ܐܬܚܙܝܘ ܠܗ̇ ܒܕܡܘܬܐ ܪܒܐ. ܒܪ ܐܢܫ̈ܝܢ
ܠܗ̇. ܠܐ ܬܕܚܠܝܢ ܐܘܦܡܝܐ ܒܡܒܝ ܚܝ. ܘܠܐ ܫܒܩܝܢ
ܠܒܝ. ܒܟܠ ܗ̇ܘܐ ܦܘܪܩܢܝ. ܚܪܒܘܬܟܝ ܚܒܪ ܡܪܒܢܐ
28,29 ܗ̇ܝ ܀ ܘܠܐ ܡܬܡܠܟܢܐ ܗܝܡܢܘܬܐ ܕܐܡ̈ܗܬܝ ܀ ܘܢܦܠ
ܥܠܝܗ̇ ܫܠܝܐ ܘܫܡܠܝܬ. ܘܒܫܠܝܐ ܗ̇ܘ ܕܠܡܫܝܚܐ ܦܫܩ
ܠܗ̇. ܗܕܐ ܬܕܡܘܪܬܐ ܠܐ ܡܬܡܠܠܢܘܬܐ ܐܬܦܠܓܪܬ
ܠܘܬܗ̇: ܐܝܟ ܕܐܦ ܠܘܬ ܢܒܝܐ ܚܒܩܘܩ ܒܓܘܒܐ: ܗ̇ܘ
ܕܒܝ ܚܒܫ ܗܘܐ ܕܢܐܟܠ ܒܪ ܪܓܫܐ ܗܘܐ ܟܠܗ ܠܘܩܒܠܐ

2 P ܕܩܒܠܬ   3 P ܪܒܬ   6 ܒܢ̈ܘܗܪܐ .... ܡܒܪܟܬܐ] P <   7 P ܡܫܒܚܝܢ   8 P ܘܡܢ ܫܠ   9 ܗ̇ܘ ܫܦܝܪܐ ܘܟܝܢܐ] P ܗ̇ܘ ܟܝܢܐ   10 ܕܗܝܡܢܘܬܐ] P ܕܕܡܝܢ ܠܗܘܢ ܠܘܬ (*sic*)   10, 11 P ܘܒܡܕܒܪܢܘܬ ܐܢ̈ܫܐ   12 P ܐܘܦܡܝܐ   13 P ܒܟܠܗ   16 ܗܕܐ] P <   18 ܟܠܗ ܠܘܩܒܠܐ] P ܟܠܘܩܒܠܐ

ܠܗܘܢ ܡܬܠܒܟܐ ܥܠ ܠܒܗܘܢ. ܕܟܡܒܪܐ ܢܣܒܗܘܢܝ ܓܝܪ
ܥܠܕܐ ܒܪ ܚܘܪܐ. ܘܢܐܚܘܕܘܢ ܒܟ̈ܘܦܝܗ. ܘܟܕ ܡܬܟܪܟܪܝܢ
ܠܗ ܘܡܚܣܢܝܢ ܠܗ: ܣܪܐܘܗܝ ܒ̈ܢܝ ܡܕܝܢܬܐ ܘܐܬܬܥܝܩܘ
ܥܠܝܗ. ܘܡܢ ܕܐܙܠܘ ܘܫܒܩܘܗ ܒܡܒܪܐ ܓܝܪ ܥ̈ܠܕܐ:
ܐܬܢܨܒܘ ܕܕܠܒܟܐ ܢܐܬܘܢ ܒ̈ܢܝ ܡܕܝܢܬܐ ܘܢܬܦܢܘܢ
ܠܗ ܘܢܦܩܘܢܝܗ. ܘܫܕܠܘ ܒܐܦܐ ܚܕܐ ܙܒܢܬܐ ܘܡܫܝܢܬܐ
ܘܐܙܕܗܪܘ ܥܠ ܬܪܥܗ: ܐܝܟ ܕܠܐ ܐܢܫ ܢܬܒܛܝܐ ܢܥܠܠ
ܒܐܦܐ ܗ̇ܝ. ܡܢ ܡܕܒܪܐ ܗ̣ܘ. ܘܐܬܢܨܒܘ ܗܘܘ ܬܘܒ
ܕܥܠ ܓܒܗ ܕܡܕܒܪܐ ܢܪܡܘܢ ܟܠܗ ܠܠܝܐ ܗ̣ܘ. ܘܠܓܒܪܐ
ܡܢ ܡܕܒܪܐ ܢܦܩܘܢܝܗ ܘܢܗܦܟܘܢܝܗ ܥܠ ܡܫܟܐ. ܘܢܕܒܪܘܢ
ܒܗ ܠܐܪ̈ܥܐ. ܡܛܠ ܕܕܢܝܐ ܪܚܝܩ ܗܘܐ ܡܢ ܐܬܪܐ
ܗ̣ܘ܀ ܘܟܕ ܥܒܕܝܢ ܗܘܘ ܥܠ ܒܒܝܬܗ ܘܦܠܘܪܦܗ̇ ܠܐ ܝܕܥ
ܥܠܝܗ. ܒܐܝܪ ܗܘܐ ܕܝܢ ܬܫܪܝܬ ܘܡܛܠ ܠܗ̇ ܪܚܡܐ
ܕܚܪܘܬܐ ܕܥܠܕܐ ܗ̇ܢܘ.܀ ܡܢܕܝܢ ܟܒܪܬ ܡܢ ܠܘܬܐ ܠܘܬ 25
ܐܠܗܐ ܘܐܡܪܬ. ܐܠܗܗ ܕܓܘܪܝܐ ܕܫܡܘܢܐ ܘܕܚܒܝܒ:

1 ܕܟܡܒܪܐ] P + ܗܘ ܕܡܟܪܬܗ 2 ܘܟܕ] L* < ܘ ܡܬܟܪܟܪܝܢ] P ܡܬܟܠܟܠܝܢ 3 P ܣܪܐܘܗܝ ܡܕܝܢܬܐ] P ܒܗ 4 P ܒܡܒܪܐ (*sic*) ܓܝܪ ܥ̈ܠܕܐ] P ܥܠܕܐ 5–6 ܐܬܢܨܒܘ....ܘܢܦܩܘܢܝܗ] P ܐܬܢܨܒܘ ܗܘܘ ܒ̈ܢܝ ܡܕܝܢܬܐ ܕܢܐܬܘܢ ܢܦܬܚܘܢ ܡܕܒܪܐ ܘܢܐܦܩܘܢܝܗ ܚܕܐ] P < 7 ܢܬܒܛܝܐ] P + ܫܠܝܐ 7–8 ܢܥܠܠ .... ܗ̣ܘ] P ܕܢܦܬܚܝܗ ܠܡܕܒܪܐ ܗ̣ܘ 8 P ܘܬܘܒ ܐܬܢܨܒܘ ܗܘܘ 9 P ܓܒܗ 10 P ܢܦܩܘܢܝܗ ܡܢ ܡܕܒܪܐ 12 P ܫܡܥܘ 14 P ܓܒܪܬ 15 ܐܠܗܗ] P ܐܠܗܐ ܘܫܡܘܢܐ ܘܚܒܝܒ P

ܒܘܕܐ ܗܘ ܕܒܡܪܐ ܕܦܩܪܬ ܒܗ ܫܦܝܪܘܬܗ ܕܒܪܝܗ:
ܐܦܩܬ ܡܢ ܫܘܕܪܗ ܘܠܡܫܬܗ ܒܒܣܡܐ ܕܡܕܪܐ: ܒܕ
ܐܡܪܬ. ܕܐܫܢܐ ܐܢ ܡܕܝܢ ܐܡܠܝܬ ܠܒܪܝ، ܘܡܢܬ.
ܘܐܢ ܕܝܢ ܘܠܐ ܗܘܝܬ ܡܕܒܪܐ ܐܢܫܝ. ܕܡܘܬܐ ܕܡܢ
ܐܠܗܐ ܡܢܬ ܒܪܝ،.܀ ܘܒܕ ܐܬܝܗܒܬ ܡܗܕܝ. ܡܪܝܟܬ
ܠܒܣܐ ܘܐܣܝܬܗ ܠܐܢܫܬ ܟܘܬܐ. ܘܒܕ ܢܦܩܬ ܡܪܬܗ
ܘܝܬܝܬ ܒܣܐ ܗܘ. ܐܦ ܗܝ ܕܡܦܩܬ ܫܢܬܐ ܕܡܘܬܐ.
ܘܒܗܘ ܠܒܘܡܟܐ ܕܦܩܪܬ ܒܗ ܢܦܠܬ. ܘܡܝܬܬ ܐܢܬܬ
24 ܠܟܘܬܐ ܘܐܬܘܩܪܬ.܀ ܘܡܢ ܒܬܪ ܥܒܕܐ ܘܡܫ̈ܒܚܝܢ
ܕܐܟܠܗ: ܒܢ̈ܝ ܠܒܣܗ ܘܐܫ̈ܝܢܗ ܕܠܟܘܬܐ ܗܝ:
ܐܬܬܒܪܘ ܐܝܟ ܐܪ̈ܘܬܐ ܘܫܘܒܚܐ ܫܠܡ ܠܗܘܢ.
ܕܗܝ ܐܒܣܢܬܐ ܕܡܦܩܬ ܠܗ ܒܣܐ ܕܫܡܐ ܕܡܘܬܐ
ܘܡܝܬܬ. ܘܡܬܝܗܒܝܢ ܗܘܘ ܒܠܝܗ ܕܢܠܡܘܢܗ ܠܒܪܢܫܐ.
ܘܡܛܠ ܕܕܢܫܐ ܪܚܡ ܗܘܐ ܡܢ ܐܬܪܐ ܗܘ: ܫܠܡ

1 ܕܦܩܪܬ] P + ܗܘܬ   P ܫܦܝܪܘܬܐ   2 P ܐܦܩܬܗ
ܡܢ ܫܘܕܪܗ] P <   3 ܕܐܫܢܐ] P < ܕ   4 ܘܠܐ] P ܠܐ
4, 5 ܕܡܢ ܐܠܗܐ] P ܕܐܠܗܐ   5 ܒܪܝ،] P <   ܐܬܝܗܒܬ
ܡܗܕܝ] P ∾   L ܡܪܝܟܬܗ   6 ܠܟܘܬܐ] P + ܗܘ
7 ܘܝܬܝܬ ܒܣܐ ܗܘ] P ܠܒܣܐ ܗܘ ܡܢ ܦܠܠܬܐ ܘܐܬܝܬܝܬ
P ܫܢܬ ܡܘܬܐ   8 ܘܒܗܘ ܠܒܘܡܟܐ] P ܘܒܠܒܘܡܟܐ
ܕܡܘܬܐ   P ܢܦܠܬ   9 ܠܟܘܬܐ] P + ܗܘ
ܥܒܕܐ] P ܐ̄   10 P ܕܗܝ ܠܟܘܬܐ   12 ܐܒܣܢܬܐ]
P pr. ܐܡܬܐ   ܕܫܡܐ] P <   14 ܘܡܛܠ ܕܕܢܫܐ]
P ܘܕܢܫܐ. ܒܠܝܗ. ܘܒܕ̈ܪܐ ܫܡ̈ܝܢܐ ܢܒܕܪܘܢ   14–1 ܫܠܡ
ܘܬܘܒ ܫܘܒܚܐ ܫܠܡ ܠܗܘܢ P [.... ܠܟܘܢ

ܐܬܬ݁ܝ، ܐܝܟܢܐ ܕܫܒܪܐ ܡܢ ܐܝܟܐ ܕܫܕܪܬܗ ܡܪܬܗ.
ܚܙܬ ܒܪܗ̇ ܕܚܝܐ ܘܦܨܝܐ ܡܢ ܗܘ ܣܡܐ ܕܡܘܬܐ.
ܘܦܓܥܐ ܒܠ ܫܘܥܬܗ ܕܚܫܝܪܐ. ܘܐܬܕܟܪܬ ܡܕܡ ܠܐ
ܡܚܝܠܐ ܗܘܬ. ܐܠܐ ܕܠܡܘܢ ܒܥܝܐ ܗܘܬ ܡܬܪܐܝܬ
ܘܪܘܚܐ ܠܬܘܕܝܬܐ ܠܡܘܕܝܢܘܬܗ̇. ܘܐܬܚܫܒܬ ܒܠܒܗ̇.
ܘܐܬܝܬ ܒܥܘܕܐ ܕܡܚܪ ܘܦܓܪܬ ܡܢ ܫܘܥܬܗ ܕܒܪܗ̇
ܣܡܐ ܗܘ ܕܡܘܬܐ: ܗ̇ܝ، ܕܐܬܚܫܠܬܗ ܗܘܬ ܗ̇ܝ،
ܠܘܬܝܬܐ. ܘܣܡܬܗ ܒܥܘܕܪܢܗ̇ ܘܒܠܚܪܬܗ ܗܘܬ
ܒܚܡܝܪܘܬܐ.܀. ܘܒܬܪ ܙܒܢܐ ܩܠܝܠ ܓܒܬ ܓܠܝܐ ܗܘ
23 ܘܐܬܘܡܒܪ ܀ ܘܡܢ ܒܬܪ ܙܒܢܐ ܩܠܝܠ ܕܒܘܝܢܗ ܕܒܪܗ̇
ܕܡܫܘܚܕܬܐ ܘܦܠܛܬܐ. ܒܥܝܕܐ ܗܘܬ ܠܗ ܚܫܝܫܬܐ
ܠܓܘܬܐ ܗܘ. ܘܩܪܡ ܗܘܘ ܠܗ ܚܒܪ̈ܘܗ̇. ܘܒܪܡܫܐ ܒܗ
ܚܫܘܟ ܐܫܟܚܬ ܠܗ̇ ܒܒܢܐ ܕܝܗܒ ܐܝܕܐ: ܕܐܬܡܣܟܢܪ
ܓܝܪ ܡܪܬܗ ܗܘ ܡܕܡ ܕܣܓܪܬ ܗ̇ܝ، ܓܝܪ ܒܪܗ ܘܢܦܫܟ
ܒܠܒܗ̇ ܒܪܚܫܗ̇. ܘܒܚܫܐ ܕܓܠܝܬܐ ܬܬܓܝܪ ܐܦ ܒܡܘܬܐ.
ܘܒܗ ܡܫܡܫܐ ܠܗܘܢ ܐܝܟ ܐܡܬܐ: ܘܡܝܩܪܐ ܠܗܘܢ.

1 LP ܐܬܬ݁ܝ، ܕܫܕܪܬܗ] P + ܗܘܬ 2 P ܠܒܪܗ̇ ܕܚܝܐ] P ܕܚܝܒ (sic) ܘܦܨܝܐ] L^{corr} ܕܦܨܝܐ (vid), P ܘܦܨܝܐ ܗܘܐ P ܣܡܐ 3 ܫܘܥܬܗ ܕܚܫܝܪܐ] P ܫܘܥܬܐ ܕܝܠܗ 4 ܕܠܡܘܢ] P < 7 ܗ̇ܝ،] P < 8 ܒܥܘܕܪܢܗ̇] P ܒܐܣܛܪ̈ܝܗ̇ ܗܘܬ] P < 9 ܒܚܡܝܪܘܬܐ] P + ܪܒܬܐ ܘܒܬܪ.... ܩܠܝܠ] P ܘ ܓܠܝܐ] P ܕܒܪܐ 13 ܠܗ̇] P + ܬܠܝܬܐ ܕܝܗܒ] P + ܠܗ̇ 14 ܗܘ ܡܕܡ] P ܗܘ ܡܐ ܗ̇ܝ،] P ܗܘܬ 15 ܬܬܓܝܪ] P ܐܬܬܓܝܪܬ ܐܦ] P + ܗ̇ܝ،

ܒܡܐ ܕܐܡܪܐ ܠܝ. ܚܘܒܐ ܡܚܝܠ ܣܘܪܚܢܐ ܘܕܚܠܬܐ
ܠܐ ܡܬܒܥܝܢ ܠܝ. ܘܟܕ ܕܟ̈ܝܘܬܐ ܣܓܝ̈ܐܬܐ ܒܪܚܡܘܬܐ
ܗܠܝܢ ܐܡܪܬ ܠܝ. ܐܡܪ ܠܗ̇ ܗܘ. ܫܠܝܚܐ ܐܢܬܝ،
ܥܠܝܗ̇. ܒܟܠܡܕܡ ܕܢܨܒܐ ܐܢܬܝ، ܕܬܫܡܫܝܢ ܫܦܝܪ،.
21 ܕܐܡܬܟܝ ܗ، ܗ̇ܝ ܀ ܗ̇ܝ ܕܝܢ ܣܒܪܬܗ̇ ܕܐܣܝܪܬܐ ܦܠܛܬ ܢܦ̈ܫܐ:
ܠܒܫܬ ܛܠܝܐ ܠܗܘܒܠ ܠܛܠܝܐ ܗ̇ܘ ܘܐܬܬܥܝܩܬ ܗܘܬ
ܕܬܟܠܠܗܘܢ،. ܘܐܬܬܕܝܪܬ ܣܡܟܐ ܦܘܠܛܐ ܕܐܡܘܬܐ.
ܕܐܡܗ، ܕܗܘܐ ܠܗ ܐܬܪܐ ܬܟܠܝܢܗ، ܠܫܒܪܐ ܗܘ
ܘܢܟܘܬ. ܦܩܕ ܒܪ ܐܠܝܐ ܗܘܬ ܒܝܬܗ̇. ܘܟܕ ܗܢ
ܡܘܬܐ: ܟܕ ܡܫܦܦ ܫܒܪܐ ܗܘ ܡܟܝ ܟܠܗ̇: ܟܕ ܡܟܪ
ܠܗ ܕܐܡܗ ܐܚܬܗ̇. ܘܫܕܪܐ ܢܦܫܗ ܟܠܗ̇. ܗ̇ܝ ܕܝܢ
ܡܫܕܪܐ ܐܬܡܟܪܬ ܣܓܝ. ܘܫܕܪܬܗ̇ ܠܐܡܗ ܠܫܘܠܡܐ
ܠܕܘܟܬܐ ܕܢܝܚܐ ܗܘܬ: ܒܟܠܬܐ ܕܢܟܘܬܐ ܡܕܡ. ܘܟܕ
ܝܕܥܬ ܕܐܡܗ ܠܐ ܦܪܝܫܐ ܗܘܬ̇. ܫܒܩܬ ܣܓܝܐ ܗܘ
22 ܕܡܘܬܐ̇ ܘܐܬܦܢܝܬܗ ܠܛܠܝܐ ܐܘ ܟܕ ܒܝܬ ܠܫܒܪܐ ܗܘ. ܘܟܕ

1 ܡܚܝܠ] P < ܣܘܪܚܢܐ] P ܣܘܪܚܢܘܬܐ
2, 3 ܒܪܚܡܘܬܐ ܗܠܝܢ] P ∼ 3 ܐܡܪܬ] P + ܗܘܬ
4 L ܫܦܝܪ 5 ܕܐܡܬܟܝ] P < ܕ ܗ̇ܝ ܕܝܢ] P ܗܕܝܢ
6 ܛܠܝܐ] P ܣܡܟܐ ܗܘܬ] P < 7 P ܦܐܡܐ
8 ܕܗܘܐ] P ܕܬܗܘܐ P ܐܬܟܠܝܢܗ، 9 ܒܝܬܗ]
P ܒܝܬܐ ܕܠܗ 10 ܗܘ] P < ܟܕ] P <
12 ܣܓܝ] P ܛܒ P ܘܫܕܪܬ 13 ܗܘܬ] P <
ܕܢܟܘܬܐ] P < 14 ܕܐܡܗ] P + ܕܫܒܪܐ ܗܘܬ]
P < P ܦܐܡܐ 15 ܠܛܠܝܐ ܐܘ ܟܕ ܒܝܬ] P <

ܗܘܬ ܒܥܡܗ̇. ܘܡܙܕܒܢܐ ܒܗ̇ ܘܡܬܦܫܩܐ ܠܗ̇ ܒܥܠܕܒܒܢ.
ܘܗ̣ܝ ܓܠܝܬܐ ܠܐ ܝܕܥܐ ܗܘܬ ܕܬܡܠܠ ܒܠܥܕܘܗ̇
ܘܬܦܝܣܝܘܗ̇ ܒܡܕܡ. ܐܠܐ ܒܟܝܐ ܗܘܬ ܟܕ ܡܬܬܢܚܐ.
ܘܦܪܝܐ ܠܬ̈ܗܘܝܐ ܠܡܘܕܥܘܗ̇. ܡܬܐܟܪܝܐ ܗܘܬ ܣܓܝ
ܕܢܡܠܠ ܥܡܗ̇ ܐܢܫ ܣܘܪܝܐܝܬ ܘܠܝܬ ܗܘܐ. ܐܠܐ ܐܢ
ܗ̇ܘ ܓܘܬܝܐ ܕܕܒܪܗ̇ ܗܘܐ ܡܢ ܐܬܪܐ ܕܣܘܪܝܐ. ܕܐܝܟ
ܕܡܢ ܢܘܓܪܐ ܕܙܒܢܐ ܕܗܘ̣ܐ ܗܘܐ ܒܐܘܪܗܝ ܝܠܦ ܗܘܐ
ܕܢܡܠܠ: ܘܟܕ ܚܙܬܗ ܗܘܬ ܓܘܬܝܬܐ ܠܓܠܝܬܐ ܕܓܠܝܐ.
ܠܐ ܝܕܥܐ ܗܘܬ ܒܠܫܢܗ̇: ܐܠܐ ܡܬܪܐܝܐ ܡܣܟܡܐ
ܗܘܬ ܒܠܫܢܗ̇ ܕܒܢ̈ܝܐ ܡܥܡܐ. ܘܬܒܥܐ ܗܘܬ ܠܗ̇ ܡܬܐܪ
20 ܡܢ ܣܠܩܗ̇ ܕܟܠ ܟܠܠܝ ܬܓܠܠܡ ܣܢ̈ܘܗ ⁘ ܘܟܕ ܡܪܒܘ ܗܘܘ
ܝܘܡ̈ܬܗ̇ ܕܓܠܝܬܐ ܕܬܐܠܕ: ܐܬܝܠܕ ܠܗ̇ ܒܪܐ ܕܟܪܐ.
ܘܕܡܝܐ ܗܘܐ ܠܐܒܘܗܝ ܛܒ. ܘܟܕ ܚܙܬܗ ܐܢܬܬ
ܓܘܬܝܐ ܠܒܪܐ ܗܘ ܕܕܡܐ ܠܒܥܠܗ̇. ܥܠܬ ܒܚܣܡܐ.
ܘܗܝ ܒܚܣܡܘܬܐ ܪܬܝܬܐ ܐܡܪܬ ܠܒܥܠܗ̇. ܚܘܪ ܘܚܙܝ

1 ܒܥܡܗ̇] P + ܕܓܠܝܬܐ ܘܡܙܕܒܢܐ] P + ܗܘܬ
2 ܒܠܥܕܘܗ̇] P ܒܥܡܗ̇ ܒܠܥܕܝܐ 3–4 ܟܕ ... ܠܡܘܕܥܘܗ̇] P <
4 P ܘܡܬܐܟܪܝܐ] ܣܓܝ] P < 5 ܥܡܗ̇ ܐܢܫ] P ∼
6 ܐܬܪܐ ܕܣܘܪܝܐ] P ܐܬܪܗ̇ ܕܐܝܟ] P *pr.* ܗܟܢܐ
7 ܕܙܒܢܐ] P < 8 ܕܢܡܠܠ] P + ܗܘܐ ܡܠܠ ܚܙܬܗ
(L *sic*)] P ܚܙܬ 9 ܡܣܟܡܐ] P ܡܫܟܚܐ 10 ܡܬܐܪ]
P *pr.* ܕܬܒܥܒܕ 11 ܘܟܕ] P + ܕܝܢ 12 P ܘܝܘܡ̈ܬܐ
ܐܬܝܠܕ] P ܗܘܐ ܗܘܐ 13 P ܕܕܡܝܐ 14 ܠܒܥܠܗ̇]
P ܠܐܒܘܗܝ 15 ܘܗܝ] P < ܗܝ P ܘܚܙܪ

ܘܦܐܝܐ: ܘܡܫܝܕܐ ܐܬܕܠܚܬ ܘܐܫܬܓܫܬ ܘܙܪܝܬ
ܕܬܫܬܐܠܗ ܠܒܒܠܗ̇. ܕܡܢ ܐܝܟܢܐ ܐܝܬܝܗ̇ ܠܫܠܡܬܐ
ܗܕܐ ܘܡܢܐ ܠܫܡܗ̇. ܘܐܝܟܢܐ ܐܬܝܗ̇. ܘܡܢܐ ܒܒܪܐ
ܒܡܟܝ. ܗ̇ܘ ܕܝܢ ܒܡ̈ܠܐ ܐܡܪ. ܕܐܡܬܝ ܗ̇ܝ ܘܐܝܬܝܬܗ̇
ܠܒܪ ܡܢ ܣܘܪܐ. ܘܒܒܬ ܘܐܡܪܬ ܠܗ. ܡܕܡܠܘ ܡܕܡܠ
ܐܝܬ. ܚܝܬܗ̇ ܒܪ ܣܘܕܐ ܕܠܐ ܕܡ̈ܝܐ ܠܐܡܗܬܐ.
19 ܘܗ̇ܘ ܬܘܒ ܦܪܝ ܠܗ̇ ܕܒܪܪܐ ܐܡܪܬ ܕܐܡܬܝ ܗܝ. ܗ̇ܝ
ܕܝܢ ܡܫܘܕܥܬܐ. ܒܪ ܢܝܚܬ ܡܕܡ ܕܓܕܫܗ̇. ܠܗܒܬ
ܢܦܫܗ̇ ܕܬܫܡܫ ܒܡܕܘܬܐ ܒܪ ܟܠܠܐ ܘܒܐܝܡܡܐ
ܠܐܠܗܗ̇ ܦܪܝܐ ܗܘܬ ܘܗܠܝܢ ܐܡܪܐ ܗܘܬ ܒܠܫܢܗ̇.
ܐܠܗܝ ܠܐ ܬܪܫܡ ܒܡܕܝܢܟ ܡܢܝ. ܣܘ̈ܕܐ ܡܪ̈ܝܐ
ܘܡܡܘ ܠܝ ܒܐܬܪܐ ܕܐܒܫܝܐ. ܬܘܕܝܐ ܦܪ̈ܥܝ ܚܝܘ
ܫܘܒܚܝ. ܘܕܘܘ ܕܒܢܐ ܕܠܚܡܘܬܝ.܀ ܗ̇ܝ ܕܝܢ ܡܪܬܗ̇
ܒܫܝܐܬܐ ܪܒܬܐ ܘܒܒܠܕܒܒܘܬܐ ܪܒܬܐ ܡܚܠܠܐ

1 ܘܦܐܝܐ] P < ܘܡܫܝܕܐ] P < ܘ 2 P ܕܬܫܬܐܠܒܘܗ̇
2 P ܕܡܢ ܐܝܟܢܐ ܗ̇ܝ 3 P ܠܐܦܝܗ̇ ܘܡܢܝܐ]
P ܘܡܘܢ 5 ܘܒܒܬ ܘܐܡܪܬ] P ܘܬܘܒ ܐܡܪܬ
6 ܕ ܣܘܕܐ] P < P ܠܕܐܡܗ̈ܬܐ 7 .... ܘܗ̇ܘ
ܐܡܪܬ] P ܗܘܐ ܦܪܥ ܕܝܢ ܗ̇ܘ 8 ܡܫܘܕܥܬܐ] P
ܠܫܠܡܬܐ P ܢܚܬ ܠܗܒܬ] P ܢܚܬܒܟ 9 ܕܬܫܡܫ
ܒܡܕܘܬܐ] P ܠܒܡܕܘܬܐ 9—10 ܗܘܬ ܦܪܝܐ .... ܒܪ]
P ܦܠܓ ܗܘܬ ܒܥܘܐ ܘܒܐܝܡܡܐ ܒܟܠܠܐ ܘܒܪ 10 ܘܗܠܝܢ]
ܘܡܪܐ 11 .ܡܢܝ .... ,ܐܠܗܝ] P < ″ܣܘ̈ܕܐ″ ܡܪ]
P ܦܪ̈ܥܝ ܕܬܘܕܝܐ 12 P ܘܡܡܘܢ 14 ܪܒܬܐ 1°]
P ܫܓܝܐܬܐ ܪܒܬܐ 2°] P ܕܠܐ ܣܓܝܐ

ܐܝܟ ܫܘ̈ܕܪܝܢ. ܗܠܘ ܦܘܪܫܐ ܕܡܘܬܒܗܘܢ: ܡܛܠ
ܐ̈ܘܪܚܐ ܠܪ̈ܟܒܐ ܕܗܘܘ ܒܗ ܠܝ ܘܠܟܝ: ܘܠܗܘ ܫܠܝܐ
ܬܘܩܦܐ ܕܒܝܫܐ ܒ̈ܥܠܕܒܒܝܗܘܢ ܕܗ̈ܘܝܐ. ܡܛܠ ܟܠ
ܪ̈ܟܒܐ ܕܢܦܩܬ ܠܝ ܒܒܝܬܐ ܕܐܘܫܦܬ ܐܝܟ ܡܪܝܚܬܐ
ܘܕܒܪܬܝ ܡܢܗܘܢ ܫܒܝܐ ܐܝܟ ܗܟܢ. ܘܟܠ ܡܪܝܗܘܢ.
17 ܚܝ ܡܠܟܐ ܒܒܒ ܐܢܬ ܒܒܝ ⁘ ܘܗܠܝܢ ܬܒܥܬ ܒܝ̈ܠܘܬܗ
ܠܒܝܬܐ ܘܡܫܘܕܥܬܐ: ܒܝ ܒܫ̈ܘܠܛܢܐ ܟܪܟܐ ܗܘܬ
ܘܗܠܝܢ ܐܡܪܝܐ. ܐܠܗܐ ܕܐܒܝ̈ ܗܘܝܘ ܠܝ ܒܐܬܪܐ
ܕܐܒܗܝ̈. ܘܫܘܒܚܝ ܘܦܪܩܝ ܡܢ ܐ̈ܝܕܘܗܝ ܕܒܢܝܐ
ܗܢܐ. ܕܦܪܒܝ ܒܢ̈ܫܐ ܫܠܝ ܠܕ̈ܪܬܐ. ܘܫܢܝܬܐ ܫܠܝ
ܕܢܚܬܐ. ܠܗܘܢ ܡܛܠ ܦܪܐ ܐܢܐ ܬ̈ܘܕܝܬܐ ܒܪ̈ܟܝ
ܚܘ ܫܐܪܘܬܐ ܕܐܬܒܝܬ ܒܝܢܪܐ ܕܒܒܝܘܬܐ. ܐܠܗܐ
ܕܐܬܠܗܝ ܠܢܘܣܦ ܘܩܘܐ ܠܗ ܠܘܬܝ ܒܐܪܟܐ ܕܡܝ̈ܬܐ.
ܠܐ ܬܪܟܢ ܒܥܝ̈ܢܝ ܡܢܝ. ܟܠܗ ܗܘ ܠܟܝ ܡܪܝ، ܟܠ
18 ܫܘܒܚܐ ܕܟ̈ܠܝ ܫܐ̈ܪܐ. ⁘⁘ ܘܒܒ ܡܢܝܚܘ ܘܟܝܠܘ ܠܒܝܬܗ:
ܚܙܬܗ ܗ̇ܝ ܐܝܬܝܗ ܕܡܠܬܐ ܠܦܠܝܛܬܐ ܕܫܦܝܪܐ

2 P ܠܪ̈ܟܒܝ P ܠܗ̇ܘ 3 ܬܘܩܦܐ] P < 4 ܕ ܒܒܝܬܐ]
P ܘ ܡܪܝܚܬܐ] P ܢܒܠܬܐ 6 ܐܢܬ] P < ܘܗܠܝܢ] P < ܘ
ܬܒܥܬ] P + ܗܘܬ 7–8 ܒܝ .... ܘܗܠܝܢ] P ܟܪܟܐ ܘܒܝ
ܒܫܘܠܛܢܐ ܗܠܝܢ 8 ܐܡܪܝܐ] P + ܗܘܬ 10 P ܒܫ̈ܢܝܬܐ
ܫܠܝ ܠܕ̈ܪܬܐ 11 ܠܗܘܢ .... ܐܢܐ] P < 13 ܕܐܬܠܗܝ
ܠܘܬܝ ...] P ܕܗܘܐ ܠܢܘܣܦ ܠܘܬܝ P ܕܡܝ̈ܬܐ 15 ܫܐ̈ܪܐ]
P + ܐܡܪ ܐܬܬܪܝ ܘܠܗܘܢ ܕܒܢܝ ܡܢܗܘܢ: ܡܫܘܕܥܐ
P ܘܟܠ ܢܒܝ 16 ܚܙܬܗ] P pr. ܘ ܗ̇ܝ] P <

ܠܒܘܫܗ ܕܥܒܕܐ ܕܠܒܝܫܐ ܗܘܬ. ܘܨܘܪܐ ܡܫܝܚܗ ܕܗܘܒܐ
ܕܐܠܗܘܬܐ ܗܘܬ: ܘܐܠܒܫܗ ܠܒܘܫܐ ܕܐܣܟܡܗܘܬܐ. ܗܘܝܘ
ܕܠܐ ܠܗ ܕܠܗ ܢܕܠܐ ܕܢܗܘܐ ܥܠܡܐ. ܕܝܢ ܐܡܪ ܠܗ
ܕܐܠܗܘܬܐ ܐܝܬ ܠܝ ܘܫܘܐ ܐܢܐ ܠܗ ܗܘܐ ܡܢ ܢܦܩܐ
ܦܓܪܐ. ܐܠܐ ܫܘܐ ܘܠܐ ܬܦܠܘܓ ܡܕܡ ܘܠܐ
ܡܕܡ ܐܢܐ ܐܢܫ ܐܠܗܐ ܕܗܘܐ ܒܢܝܢܐ ܘܐܠܗܐ ܫܘܬܐ
ܒܝܫܐ ܫܘܬܐ ܐܝܬ. ܡܢ ܒܗܘܢ ܘܡܢ ܟܠ ܥܒܘܕܗ.
16 ܕܡܝܕܥܐ ܐܝܬܝܗܘܢ ܒܐܬܪ. ܘܟܕ ܗܠܝܢ ܫܡܥܬ
ܠܠܒܬܐ ܐܬܬܢܝܚܬ ܡܕܡ ܐܠܗܐ ܘܐܬܪܚܡܬ ܥܠܗ
ܒܒܬܘܠܗ. ܟܕ ܦܪܩܐ ܥܠ ܐܦܘܗ ܘܥܠ ܚܕܘܗ. ܘܕܪܫܐ
ܒܦܪܐ ܒܢܫܗ ܘܒܐܦܘܗ. ܘܗܠܝܢ ܐܡܪܐ ܗܘܬ ܠܗ
ܡܫܒܚܬܐ ܠܐܠܗܐ ܗܘ ܟܕ ܒܟܝܐ ܗܘܬ. ܡܒܪܟܐ
ܦܓܪܗ ܒܒܪܐ. ܡܪܝܐ ܒܒܝܬ ܟܐܪܝ ܘܟܕܝ ܐܒܫܝܘܬܝ.
ܡܒܪܟܐ ܦܓܪܗ ܠܫܦܝܪܐ ܕܒܐܝܡܡܐ ܒܪܝ. ܒܢ
ܚܐܪܐ. ܘܟܠܒܬ ܠܝ ܕܐܝܡܬܐ ܐܢܐ ܘܒܕܝܠܬܝ ܒܢܘܪܐ
ܕܒܕܘܬܐ. ܘܠܐ ܦܠܓܠܬܝ ܒܫܘܦܐ ܠܠܒܝܫܐ. ܗܠܝܢ

1 ܠܒܘܫܐ ܡܫܝܚܐ ܕܗܘܒܐ] P + ܘܗܘ 2 P ܠܒܘܫܐ ܕܐܣܟܡܗܘܬܐ (= *σχῆμα δουλικόν* 𝔊)] Pcorr ܕܐܣܟܡܗܘܬܐ (P*vid ////ܕܐܪ), Lnunc ܕܐܪܟܠܘܬܐ *on eras.* 4 ܗܐ] P < 5 ܦܓܪܐ] P ܕܫܪܝܐ ܦܓܪܐܬܐ L ܫܘܬܦ ܘܠܐ 2°] P ܘܐ 6 ܐܢܫ .... ܕܗܘܝ] P ܒܢܝܢܐ ܡܕܡ ܕܗܘܐ 7 ܒܗܘܢ] P + ܕܐܠܗܘܬܐ 8 L ܗܠܝܢ ܗܠܝܢ 10 P ܒܒܬܘܠܬܐ 12 ܗܘܬ] P < 13 ܟܐܪܝ ܘ] P < 14 P ܕܐܝܡܬܐ 15 ܘܟܠܒܬ] P ܕܟܠܒܬ: ܦܓܪܗ ܡܒܪܟܐ
16 P ܒܫܘܦܝ

ܠܝܬܘܗܝ ܕܓܠܐ. ܕܗܒ ܠܗ ܒܪܬܐ ܫܠܐ ܒܫܡܐ ܕܒܪܐ
ܥܠ ܗܠܝܢ ܦܘܪ̈ܥܢܐ. ܘܐܝܬ ܕܪܟܬ ܘܗܘܝܘ ܐܡܗܐ ܕܐܦ
14 ܦܩܕ ܐܝܬ ܠܘܬܗ ܀ ܠܗܘܢ ܕܝܢ ܠܐܘܪ̈ܚܐ ܡܩܒܠܢܝܬܐ ܗܘܬ
ܒܪ ܐܚܪ̈ܢܐ ܒܟܢܐ ܐܝܟ ܡܢܗܘܢ ܢܝܫܗܘܢ ܕܐܠܗܐ
ܘܠܗ ܒܥܢܗ ܘܡܘܡܝܐ ܠܗ ܒܐܬܪܐ ܕܐܒܫܢܐ. ܕܠܐܠܗܐ
ܘܠܗܘܢ ܗܢܝܬ ܒܠܝܗ. ܘܦܩܕ ܗܘ ܠܓܘܬܐ ܘܐܡܪܗ
ܐܚܕܗ ܘܕܒܪܗ ܡܢ ܠܐܘܣܛܒܐ ܕܗܘܪܐ ܘܕܪ̈ܚܐ ܒܗ
ܐܡܪ. ܕܐܝܟ ܕܗܘܝܐ ܐܢܐ ܒܥܢܗ ܘܦܩܕ ܐܢܐ ܠܘܬܗ
ܢܗܘܐ ܐܠܗܐ ܒܥܒܕ. ܗܐ ܗܠܝܢ ܡܕܒܪ̈ܢܐ ܚܝ̈ܒܝܢ ܕܠܐ
ܡܚܝܒ ܐܢܐ ܠܗ. ܘܓܠܝܗ ܒܠܚܘܕ ܘܫܬܘ ܡܢ ܬܡܢ.
ܐܡܬܗ ܕܝܢ ܒܫܢܐ ܡܕܝܢܬܐ ܘܒܒܒܢܐ ܬܒܝܒܐ ܒܠܠܝܐ
ܘܒܐܝܡܡܐ ܐܝܬܝܗ ܗܘܬ܆ ܕܡܢ ܒܚܝ̈ܠܐ ܘܫܝܬܐ
15 ܕܒܪܬܗ ܐܬܓܠܝܬ ܗܘܬ ܀. ܘܒܪ ܫܢܬ ܓܠܝܬܐ ܒܗ
ܠܓܘܬܐ ܗܘ ܘܐܙܠܗ ܗܘܘ ܦܫܝܫܢܐ ܡܕܝܢ̈ܬܐ܆ ܘܡܟܒܫܘ
ܗܘܘ ܠܡܕܝܢܬܐ ܕܠܗ ܐܪܝܢ ܗܘܘ ܟܠ ܚܕ ܡܫܡܫܢܐ
ܗܕܝܡ ܡܢ ܒܠܝܗ ܐܝܟ ܕܒܥܐ ܡܫܒܠܢܐ. ܘܐܫܠܝܗ

1 ܕܓܠܐ] P ܒܕܒܐ   2 ܗܠܝܢ] P ܕܗܠܝܢ ܒܪܡܫܗܘܢ
2–3 ܠܘܬܗ .... ܘܐܝܬ] P .ܐܝܬ ܢܕܒ ܘܦܪܣܘ ܘܐܝܬ
ܐܝܟ ܕܗܘܐ ܐܝܬ ܒܥܢܗ   4–5 ܘܠܗ .... ܒܟܢܐ]
P ܕܘܠܗ   5 P ܘܡܘܡܝܘ   5–6 ܒܠܝܗ ... ܕܠܐܠܗܐ]
P <   8 ܠܘܬܗ .... ܘܦܩܕ] P <   9 ܚܝ̈ܒܝܢ] P ܚܝ̈ܒ
10 ܒܠܚܘܕ] P <   ܡܢ ܬܡܢ] P <   12–13 ܗܘܬ .... ܕܡܢ]
P ܕܒܪܬܗ ܘܫܝܬܐ ܒܚܝ̈ܠܐ ܡܢ ܕܐܬܦܪܫܬ   13 ܘܒܪ]
P ܒܪ ܕܝܢ   15 ܗܘܘ .... ܠܡܕܝܢܬܐ] P ܠܡܕܝܢܬܗ ܕܒܠܠܐ
ܚܕ ܡܫܡܫܢܐ] P ~   16 ܗܕܝܡ] P <   P ܕܒܥܐ ܢܒܠܐ

ܘܡܫܒܚܬܗ ܒܪܬܗ ܒܢ̈ܫܐ. :· ܘܡܢ ܒܬܪ ܕܒܢܐ ܢܦܩ
ܐܠܗܐ ܘܗܘܐ ܫܝܢܐ. ܘܫܪܬ ܕܢܦܩܘ ܗܢܐ ܒܥܠܡܐ
ܠܐܬܪܗ ܡܢ ܫܪܒܐ ܕܗܝܠܘܢ ܕܒܡܫܗ ܠܒܬ̈ܘܠܬܐ.
ܘܐܬܦܠܓܬ ܕܐܦ ܠܐܘܦܡܝܐ ܗ̇ܝ ܕܢܫܒ ܒܢ̈ܫܐ ܢܕܒܪ
12 ܒܡܡܗ ܠܒܪ ܕܢܦܫ. ܘܫܪܝܬ ܡܬܚܢܢܐ ܐܡܡܗ. ܕܠܒܠܡ
ܗܕܐ ܠܐ ܬܗܘܐ: ܘܒܪܬܗ ܒܫܡܗ ܠܐ ܬܐܙܠ ܡܛܠ
ܕܟܠܘ ܕܢܚܫܗ :· ܘܟܕ ܩܠܝܢ ܐܬܒܩܪܬ: ܘܡܬܚܡܬܐ
ܩܪܝܐܐ ܠܗ ܗܕܐ ܐܘܣܦܬ ܬܐܓܪܐ ܠܢܪܬܐ ܐܙܕܒܢܬ.
ܘܠܐ ܐܬܟܢܫܬ ܕܠܒܪܬܗ ܬܫܘܒ. ܘܬܦܩ ܡܢ ܡܐܘܠܬܐ
13 ܕܒܡܡܗ. ܘܟܕ ܦܫܩܬ ܠܗ ܥܠ ܦܘܪܫܢܐ ܕܢܫܬܡܥܬܗ:
ܕܒܪܬ ܠܢܬܘܢܗ ܒܕܒܐ ܘܠܒܪܬܗ. ܘܐܫܟܚܬ ܐܝܟ ܠܒܢܬ
ܗܕܐ ܕܦܪ̈ܫܐ ܘܡܬܕ̈ܝܢܐ. ܠܦܪܐ ܘܫܡܘܢܐ ܘܝܒܢ.
ܘܡ̈ܠܝܢ ܗ̇ܘ ܒܕ̈ܡܒܐ ܢܫܝܠܬܐ ܐܡܗܐ ܡܢ ܒܪܬܐ
ܕܠܗ.·: ܘܟܕ ܫܡܥܝܢ ܠܘܬܗܘܢ ܡܢ ܕܡܒܐ: ܡܪܢܬ
ܐܡܗ ܕܡܠܬܐ ܘܠܒܬܗ ܒܡܡܢܗ ܘܫܡܥܬܗ ܠܒܠ ܡܢ
ܠܫܘܡܟܐ ܕܠܗܘܢ ܕܡܬ̈ܕܝܢܐ. ܒܝ ܐܡܬܪܐ ܗܘܬ

1 P ܘܡܫܒܚܬ ܠܗ   2 ܘܫܪܬ] P ܘܟܕ ܫܪܬ ܠܗ
ܒܥܠܡܐ] P ܡܢܪܝܢܐ   3–5 ܡܢ ..... ܕܢܦܫ] P <
5 ܘܫܪܝܬ] P < ܘ   5 ܐܡܡܗ] P + ܕܦܠܝܬܐ   5–6 ܕܠܒܠܡ
.... ܬܐܙܠ] P ܕܠܐ ܬܐܙܠ ܒܪܬܗ ܒܫܡܗ   7–10 ܘܟܕ
.... ܕܢܫܬܡܥܬܗ] P ܘܟܕ ܠܐ ܐܫܟܚܬ ܕܬܦܠܓܝܗ ܡܢܗ
ܘܐܙܕܒܢܬ ܠܗ   12 ܕܦܪ̈ܫܐ ܘܡ̈ܬܕܝܢܐ″] P ܦܪ̈ܫܐ. ܡ̈ܬܕܝܢܐ
13, 14 ܡܢ ܒܪܬܐ ܕܠܗ] P ܘܒܪܬܗ   14 ܫܡܥܝܢ
..... ܕܡܒܐ] P ܠܘܬ   16 P ܕܦܪ̈ܫܐ ܡܘ̈ܕܝܢܐ
ܗܘܬ] P ܠܗ

ܠܗ: ܙܠ ܠܟܝ ܡܢܝ. ܘܗܘ ܬܘܒ ܡܬܬܙܝܥ ܗܘܐ ܒܠܒܗ.
ܟܕ ܢܠܦ ܗܘܐ ܒܗ ܫܘ̈ܕܠܐ ܐܦ ܡܘ̈ܗܒܬܐ ܀ ܘܟܕ 10
ܦܝܣܐܝܬ ܬܒܥܗ̇: ܘܒܡܘ̈ܗܒܬܐ ܦܝ̈ܣܐܐ ܒܚܝܠܐ ܗܘܢܐ
ܥܢܫ ܗܘܐ ܠܗ̇. ܐܙܕܒܢܬ ܐܝܟ ܐܢܬܬܐ ܡܣܟܠܬܐ̇
ܘܐܬܪ̈ܦܝܬ ܒܬܪܒܝܬܗ̇ ܕܒ̇ ܐܡܪܐ ܕܐܠܗܐ ܕܝ̈ܬܡܐ
ܘܕܐܪ̈ܡܠܬܐ ܬܐ ܠܒܝܬܝ. ܐܠܗܝ ܡܟܝܠ ܠܟܝ ܫܘܒܪܢܐ
ܗܢܝ. ܕܠܟܝ ܗܘ ܒܠܚܘܕܝܟܝ ܚܠܐ. ܘܫܘܝܐ ܙܒܢܐ ܗܘܐ
ܒܢܝܬ ܐܡܪܗ̇ ܕܛܠܝܬܐ ܠܡܘܬܐ ܗܘ̇ ܕܒ̇ ܐܡܪܐ. ܕܠܐ
ܡܫܟܚܐ ܐܢܐ ܕܐܦܪܘܫ ܒܝܢܬܝ ܡܢܝ: ܗܢܐ ܒܠܗ
ܪܘܫܡܐ. ܗܘ ܕܝܢ ܡܚܒܐ ܗܘܐ ܒܐܠܗܐ ܕܠܐ ܠܐ ܡܫܢܝܐ
ܐܢܐ ܠܗ̇ ܡܢ ܐܬܕܟܪ ܘܠܬܘܒ ܡܬܬܘܬܒܝܢ. ܀ ܘܟܕ 11
ܫܡܥܬ ܐܢܬܬܐ ܠܡܘܗܒܬܗ ܕܒܥܠܝ. ܐܬܪܚܒܬ ܠܡܫܡܠܝܘ
ܨܒܝܢܗ. ܘܗܝܕܝܢ ܡܚܕܐ ܒܓܕܘ ܒܬܒܐ ܕܦܪܝܫܬܐ

1 ܠܗ] P + ܕܐܢܬܝ, ܐܢܬܬܐ ܡܫܝܚܝܬܐ ܘܗܘ] P ܗܘ ܕܝܢ ܡܬܬܙܝܥ P 2 ܟܕ ... ܐܦ] P ܘܡܦܝܣܐ 3 ܦܝܣܐܝܬ] P ܦܝܣ 3–4 ܘܒܡܘ̈ܗܒܬܐ .... ܠܗ̇] P < 4 ܐܢܬܬܐ] P < 5 ܒܬܪܒܝܬܗ̇] P < ܕܐܠܗܐ] P < ܕ 6 ܐܠܗܝ] P ܐܠܗܐ ܡܟܝܠ] P + ܐܢܐ (sic) 7 ܗܢܐ] P < ܗܘ ܒܠܚܘܕܝܟܝ] P < ܙܒܢܐ] P ܦܝܣܐܐ 8 ܒܢܝܬ] P ܒܢܬ 10 ܒܐܠܗܐ] P ܕܐ 10–11 ܕܠܐ ..... ܀] P ܡܘ̈ܗܒܬܐ ܚܫܝ̈ܚܬܐ ܗܘ̇ ܠܗ̇ ܠܗ. ܘܠܐܠܗܐ ܐܬܩܢ̈ܝ ܡܢ ܐܬܪ ܐܢܐ ܘܗܘ. ܗܘܕܝܢ ܟܕ 11 ܘܟܕ] P ܘܬܘܡܝܢ ܬܪܝܢ ܠܬܘܒ ܀ ܗܠܝܢ ܡܘ̈ܗܒܬܐ ܚܫܝ̈ܚܬܐ 12 ܠܡܘ̈ܗܒܬܗ] P ܕܒܥܠܐ 12–13 ܐܬܪܚܒܬ ... ܨܒܝܢܗ] P ܐܬܪܚܒܬ 13 ܘܗܝܕܝܢ ܡܚܕܐ] P ܘ P ܒܬ̈ܒܐ

7

ܡܫܪܝܠ ܗܘܐ ܠܗ̇. ܘܢܛܝܠ ܗܘܐ ܐܦ ܕܗܒܐ ܘܡܫܘܚܐ
ܗܘܐ ܠܚܒܝܫܗ̇ ܒܪ ܡܬܦܪܘܣ ܒܟܠ ܫ̈ܒܝܠܝܢ. ܕܬܬܠ ܠܗ ܗ̇ܝ
9 ܒܪܬ ܚܐܪܐ ܒܪܬܗ̇ ⁛ ܗ̇ܝ ܕܝܢ ܦܠܫܬܗ̇ ܠܒܪܬܗ̇ ܕܐܦܠܐ
ܢܣܒܗ̇ ܒܪ ܐܡܪܬ ܠܗ. ܒܒܪܬܐ ܡܢܐ ܠܝ ܘܠܟ· ܡܢܐ
ܫܦܝܪ ܐܢܬ ܠܝ: ܕܐܢܬܬܐ ܐܢ̇ܬܝ، ܡܣܟܝܢܬܐ ܘܐܪܡܠܬܐ.
ܘܠܐ ܫܦܝܪ ܡܫܥܒܕܐ ܐܢܐ ܕܗܘܐ ܐܚܝܕ. ܗܘ ܕܝܢ ܡܠܐ
ܗܘܐ ܢܒܠܐ ܒܡܣܟܢܘܬܗ ܘܐܫܬܘܕܝ، ܠܗ̇ ܫܟܝܪܬܐ ⁛
ܗ̇ܝ ܕܝܢ ܬܘܒ ܐܡܪܬ ܠܗ: ܘܐܝܟܢ ܡܫܟܚܐ ܕܗܕܐ
ܬܗܘܐ: ܕܟܡܐ ܢ̈ܫܝܢ ܐܢܬܬܐ ܐܝܬ ܠܟ ܒܐܬܪܟ
ܘܒ̈ܢܝܐ. ܗ̇ܘ ܕܝܢ ܡܦܢܝܐ ܠܬܒܥܝܬܗ̇ ܢܗܦܟܐ ܗܘܐ.
ܒܪ ܦܫܛܐ ܗܘܐ ܒܡܗܝܡܢܘܬܐ ܕܒܐܠܗܐ ܕܫܠܝܚܐ. ܕܠܐ
ܡܬܘܡ ܐܢܬܬܐ ܫܩܠ ܐܢܐ ܘܠܐ ܒܢ̈ܝܐ ܐܝܬ ܠܝ.
ܘܐܝܬ، ܕܗܒܐ ܗ̇ܘ ܕܢܛܠ ܘܦܪܩ ܡܙܡܢܝ ܒܪ ܐܚܪ̈ܝ.
ܕܗܘܐ ܚܕ، ܕܠܝܬ ܠܝ ܐܢܬܬܐ: ܕܗܘܐ ܕܗܒܐ ܗܘܐ ܫܟܝܚܐ
ܠܒܪܬܗ، ܢܫܠܬ: ܘܫܠܡܬܐ ܫܟܝܪܬܐ ܝܗܒ ܐܢܐ ܠܗ̇ ⁛
ܘܬܘܒ ܐܡܪܬ ܠܗ. ܒܒܪܬܐ ܡܢܐ ܫܦܝܪ ܐܢܬ

1 ܗܘܐ (*after* ܘܢܛܝܠ)] P < 1–2 ܘܡܫܘܚܐ .... ܫ̈ܒܝܠܝܢ] P ܘܐܬܦܪܘܣ ܡܢ ܟܠ ܟܬ̈ܒܝܢ 2 ܗ̇ܝ] P ܗ̇ܝ، 3 ܗ̇ܝ ܕܝܢ] P ܗ̇ܝ، 4 ܡܢܐ ܠܝ ܘܠܟ] P < 5 ܕܐܢ̇ܬܝ، ܐ″] P ܐܪ″ ܘܡܟܝܟ″ 6 ܘܠܐ ܫܦܝܪ .... ܐܚܝܕ] P ܕܗܘܐ ܠܐ ܡܫܥܒܕܐ ܐܢܐ ܕܐܚܝܕ ܡܠܐ] P *pr.* ܒܪ 7 ܘܐܫܬܘܕܝ،] P ܒܪ ܐܫܬܘܕܝ، (*sic*) 8, 9 P ܗܕܐ ܕܬܗܘܐ 11 ܒܪ .... ܕܫܠܝܚܘܬ] P < 12 ܡܬܘܡ] P < 13 ܘܐܝܬ، LP*] P *corr.* + ܠܝ 14 ܕܗܘܐ] P < 15 ܢܫܠܬ] P *pr.* ܘ ܢܣܒܬ 16 ܘܬܘܒ] P ܗ̇ܝ ܕܝܢ ܬܘܒ ܐܢܬܬܐ

ܒܡܐܐܝܬ ܕܠܐ ܢܣܝܢܗ̇ ܠܒܪܬܐ ܗ̇ܘ ܚܒܠܐ. ܕܠܘܬܗ̇ ܕܝܢ
ܕܓܘܬܝܐ ܐܝܬܘܗܝ، ܗܘܐ ܝܕܥܗ̇ ܐܘܦܡܝܐ. ܘܒܚܙܬܗ̇
ܠܒ ܝܕܥܐ ܗܘܬ ܀ ܘܟܕ ܕܝܢ ܢܦܩܬ ܦܓܥܐ ܕܒܝܬܐ 6
ܗܘܐ ܠܘܬܗܘܢ ܠܒܪܬܐ ܗ̇ܘ. ܟܕ ܕܝܢ ܘܡܚܝ ܚܒܠ ܒܝܬܗ̇
ܠܓܠܝܬܐ. ܘܒܪܟܬܗ̇ ܠܒ ܐܬܟܢܫܬ. ܘܒܪܚܡܬܗ̇
ܐܫܬܘܕܥܬ ܢܦܫܗ̇: ܘܡܢ ܗ̇ܘ ܕܝܢ ܓܒܪ، ܗܘܐ ܕܒܬܘ̈ܠܐ 7
ܡܫ̈ܝܚܬܐ ܘܪ̈ܒܒܬܐ ܢܛܠܝܗ̇ ܠܐܡܗ̇ ܕܓܠܝܬܐ: ܐܡܪܐ
ܕܠܐܘܦܡܝܐ ܒܪܬܗ̇ ܬܬܠ ܠܗ ܠܡ ܒܥ̈ܪܐ ܕܬܗܘܐ ܠܗ
ܠܐܢܬܬܐ. ܗ̇ܝ ܕܝܢ ܡܗܝܡܢܘܬܐ ܐܡܗ̇. ܟܕ ܝܕܥܬ ܠܒ
ܐܬܬܥܝܪܬ: ܘܡܬܕܚܠܐ ܗܘܬ ܒܗ. ܘܠܐ ܡܫܟܚܐ ܗܘܬ
ܡ̈ܠܘܗܝ. ܗ̇ܘ ܕܝܢ ܠܒܪܐ ܗ̇ܘ ܒܥܝܐ: ܠܐ ܫ̈ܠܐ ܗܘܐ
ܡܢ ܕܒܥܐ ܗܘܐ ܠܗ̇ ܒܬܘ̈ܠܐ ܡ̈ܬܠܝܬܐ ܕܐܝܟ ܗܠܝܢ.
ܘܐܝܬ ܐܡܗ̇، ܕܒܡܫܡܫܬܐ ܦܓܥ ܗܘܐ ܒܗ̇. ܘܐܝܬ ܐܡܗ̇، 8
ܕܒܬܘ̈ܠܐ ܕܒܡܫܡܫܢܘܬܐ ܘܕܝܘܠܦܢܐ. ܘܒܡܫܡ̈ܫܢܘܬܐ ܫܦܝ̈ܪܬܐ

1 ܒܡܐܐܝܬ] P ܐܡܝܢܐܝܬ 1–2 ܕܠܘܬܗ̇ ... ܐܘܦܡܝܐ] P ܘܠܘܬܗ̇ ܠܓܠܝܬܐ ܝܕܥܗ̇ ܗܘܬ ܐܘܦܡܝܐ 2, 3 P ܗ̇ܘ، 3–6 ܘܟܕ .... ܐܫܬܘܕܥܬ] ܠܓܠܝܬܐ ܝܕܥܐ ܗܘܬ ܟܕ ܕܝܢ ܘܚܙܬܗ̇ ܠܓܠܝܬܐ ܗ̇، ܘܒܪܟܬܗ̇. ܘܐܫܬܘܕܥܬ P 6 ܢܦܫܗ̇] P + ܒܬܪܗ̇ 6–7 ܘܡܢ ܗܘܕܝܢ .... ܠܐܡܗ̇] ܘܓܒܪ، ܗܘܐ ܪܒܐ ܥܘܕܠܐ ܠܐܡܗ̇ P 7–8 ܐܡܪܐ .... ܒܥܪܐ] ܒܬ̈ܠܐ. ܕܬܬܠ ܠܗ ܒܪܬܗ̇ ܒܥܪܐ. P 8, 9 ܕܬܗܘܐ ܠܗ ܠܐܢܬܬܐ] P < 9–10 ܐܡܗ̇ .... ܐܬܬܥܝܪܬ: ܘ] P < 11 ܗܘ ܒܥܝܐ] P < 11 ܫ̈ܠܐ] P ܬܐܢܝ 12 ܒܬܘ̈ܠܐ .... ܗܠܝܢ] P < 14 ܕܒܬܘ̈ܠܐ ܕܒܡܫܡܫܢܘܬܐ ܘܕܝܘܠܦܢܐ] P ܕܒܡܥܘܕܢܐ

ܠܐ ܬܬܟܣܐ ܒܫ̈ܢܝܟܘܢ ܬܫܥܝܬܐ ܕܡܠܟܘܬܐ ܗܕܐ
4 ܬܫܒܘܚܬܐ: ܡܛܠ ܦܘܪܥܢܘܬܐ ܕܗܘ̇ ܕܐܬܟܬܒ ܀.܀. ܒܫܢܬ
ܫ̈ܒܥܡܐܐ ܘܫܒܥ ܒܡܢܝ̣ܢܐ ܕܝ̈ܘܢܝܐ: ܢܦ̣ܩܘ ܗܘܘ
ܗܘ̈ܢܝܐ ܘܫܒ̣ܘ ܫܒ̣ܝܬܐ ܘܐܝܬܝܘܗ̇ ܠܐܬܪܐ. ܘܐܬ̇ܘ
ܒܪ̈ܘܡܝܐ ܠܐܘܪܗܝ. ܘܠܐ ܢܦ̣ܩ ܐܕܝ، ܐܣܛܪܛܠܛܝܣ ܕܒܗ̇ܘ
ܙܒܢܐ ܠܒܐܬܐ ܕܬܦܘܩ ܠܘܩܒܠܗܘܢ. ܡܛܠ ܢܒ̣ܠܐ
ܕܓܒ̣ܪܘܬܐ. ܘܡܛܠ ܗܕܐ ܚܠܬܒ̣ ܢܒ̣ܥܘ ܫ̈ܒܠܘܬܐ
5 ܕܪ̈ܗܘܡܝܐ ܘܝܬܒ̣ܘ ܒܐܘܪܗܝ، ܘܒܢܐ ܀ ܠܒܒܪ̇ܐ ܕܢܚ
ܠܒܘܬܐ ܡܢܪ̇ ܢܦܫܐ: ܡܢܗ ܕܫܠܝܐ ܗܘ̇ ܕܪ̈ܗܘܡܝܐ:
ܫܪܐ ܗܘܐ ܒܒܝܬܐ ܥܠ ܐܢܬܬܐ ܚܕܐ ܐܪܡܠܬܐ
ܡܗܝܡܢܬܐ ܕܫܡܗ̇ ܣܘܦܝܐ: ܘܠܗܕܐ ܐܝܬ ܗܘܐ ܒܪܬܐ
ܚܕܐ ܒܬܘܠܬܐ ܡܬܡܟܬܐ ܘܚܣܝܕܬܐ ܕܠܗ̇. ܘܡܗܝܪܐܝܬ
ܘܦܪܝܫܐܝܬ ܐܚܝܕܐ ܗܘܬ ܠܗ̇ ܐܡܗ̇. ܘܐܝܟ ܕܦܐܝ̇ܐ
ܒܠܚܘܕܝܗ̇ ܢܦܩܘܬܐ ܡܪܟܢܐ ܗܘܬ ܠܗ̇. ܘܡܛܦܪܢܐ ܗܘܬ ܠܗ̇

1—2 ″ܬܫ .... ܬܫܒܘܚܬܐ] P ܗܕܐ ܬܫܥܝܬܐ ܬܢܝܢܬܐ
2 ܡܛܠ .... ܕܐܬܟܬܒ] P ܡܛܠ ܡܦܩܢܘܬܐ ܕܡܠܟܘܬܗ
4 ܗܘ̈ܢܝܐ P (= 𝔊)] L *in marg., and now in txt. but on an illegible erasure: see* pp. 52, 74   ܘܫܒ̣ܘ .... ܠܐܬܪܐ] P ܠܒܝܬ ܪ̈ܘܡܝܐ. ܘܐܚܪܒܘ ܐܬܪܐ ܘܫܒ̣ܘ ܫܒ̣ܝܬܐ   5 P ܐܣܛܪܛܝܠܐܛܝܣ   6 P ܠܒܐܬ̈ܐ   8 P ܕܪ̈ܘܡܝܐ   ܘܒܢܐ] P + ܘܣܓܝܐܐ   9 ܠܒܘܬܐ] P ܢܚ (*sic*)   ܗܘ̇ ܕܪ̈ܗܘܡܝܐ] P <   10 ܒܒܝܬܐ ܥܠ] P ܝܚܕ
11 ″ܡܗ] P *pr.* ܘ   ܕܫܡܗ̇] P + ܗܘܐ   11—13 ܘܠܗܕܐ .... ܐܡܗ̇] P ܘܐܝܬ ܗܘܐ ܠܗ̇ ܒܪܬܐ ܒܬܘ̄ ܡܬܕܒܪܢܝܬܐ. ܘܡܗܝܪܐ ܗܘܬ ܒܗ̇ ܐܡܗ̇   13—14 ܘܐܝܟ ... ܠܗ̇.] P ܘܡܪܟܢܐ ܗܘܬ ܠܗ̇ ܒܠܚܘܕܝܗ̇ ܢܦܩܘܬܐ.

ܘܠܙܪܘܣ ܗܘ̇ ܕܒܝܬܐ ܡܕܝܢܬܐ ܕܝܠܗ̇ ܕܐܘܪܗܝ. ܕܐܝܬܘܗܝ
ܗܘܐ ܦܪܡܘܢܝܐ ܒܗܝܟܠܐ ܡܕܝܢܐ ܕܒܢܝܬ ܫܘ̈ܕܝܢܐ.
ܗܘ̣ ܐܫܠܡ ܠܗ ܬܫܡܫܬܐ ܕܬܕܒܘܪܬܐ ܗܕܐ ܕܗܘܬ
ܒܝܘܡܬܗ̣. ܐܝܟ ܕܝܠܦ ܡܢ ܦܘܡܗ̇ ܕܛܠܝܬܐ ܘܕܐܡܗ̇:
ܡܢ ܒܬܪ ܕܥܒܕ ܠܗ̇ ܐܠܗܐ ܦܘܪܩܢܐ ܘܦܢ̇ܬ ܠܐܬܪܗ̇
ܘܠܒܝܬ ܐܒ̈ܘܗ̇: ܒܝܕ ܒܥܘܕܪܢܐ ܘܚܝܠܐ ܕܣܗܕܘܬ
ܓܒ̈ܝܗܘܢ ܕܩܕܝܫܐ ܘܡܘ̈ܕܝܢܐ ܫܪܪܐ ܘܡܬܬܚܝܢܝܢ
ܒܠܒܕ. ܠܗ̇ ܕܒܗ ܥܒܕ ܗܟܢܐ ܗܘ ܡܬܬܪܐ: ܕܢܛܠ
ܕܢܦܫܐ ܦܘ̣ܩܕܢ ܘܢܬܛܪܘܢ: ܘܠܐ ܢܫܠܡ ܠܕܪܐ ܕܒܬܪܗ
ܐܬܝܢ: ܦܘܪܩܢܐ ܕܬܕܒܘܪܬܐ ܗܕܐ ܙܒܢܬܐ: ܕܒܝܕ 3
ܡܒܪܘܬܐ ܕܒܪܝܟܘܬܗܘܢ ܕܣܗ̈ܕܐ ܘܡ̈ܬܠܒܠܒܢܐ ܫܘ̈ܕܝܢܐ
ܥܒܕ ܘܫܒ̣ܩܐ. ܘܒܠ ܕܬܒܠ ܗܘܐ ܕܒܗ ܬܪܝܨܘܬܐ
ܫܪܝܪ. ܘܫܪܪܐ ܐܡ̣ܪܬ. ܐܫܠܡܗ̇ ܠܗ ܠܬܫܡܫܬܐ ܗܕܐ
ܐܝܟ ܕܒܝ̈ܐ ܗܘܐ ܒܚܝܠܐ ܕܐܠܗܐ. ܘܡܛܠ ܕܡܠܬܐ
ܦܫܝܛܬܐ ܗܝ. ܘܗܕܝܘܛܬܐ ܘܪܒܢܝܗ ܕܣܒܐ ܡܫܝܢ.

1 ܕܝܠܗ̇] P < 2 ܒܗܝܟܠܐ] P ܒܒܝܬܐ 3 ܗܘ̣] P ܕܗܘ̣ܘ ܕܬܕܒܘܪܬܐ ܗܕܐ] P ~ 4 ܕܝܠܦ] P + ܗܘܐ 6 ܘܚܝܠܐ] P + ܐܠܗܐ 7 ܘܡܘ̈ܕܝܢܐ] P < ܘ ܫܪܪܐ] P ܫ̈ܪܝܪܐ ܘܡܬܬܚܝܢܝܢ] P ܘܡܬ̈ܚܝܢ (sic) 8 P ܒܠܒܕܝܢ 8, 9 ܠܗ̇ .... ܘܢܬܛܪܘܢ] P ܘܥ̣ܒܕ ܗܟܢܐ ܗܘܐ ܡܬܬܪܐ ܕܢܛܪܘܢ ܘܢܬܛܪܘܢ ܘܢܦܫܐ 9, 10 ܕܒܬܪܗ] P ܒܬܪܗ ܕܐܬܝܢ ܘܠܕܪ̈ܬܐ 11 P ܕܡ̈ܬܠܒܠܒܢܐ ܫܘ̈ܕܝܢܐ ܘܡܫܘ" 12 ܘܒܠ ܕ] P ܘܡܛܠ ܕ 13 ܒܡ ܬܪ"] P < ܫܪܝܪ ܘ 15 P ܦܫܝܛܬܐ ܘܗܕܝܘܛܬܐ

⁘ ܬܫܥܝܬܐ ܕܐܘܦܝܡܝܐ ⁘

1 ܬܫܥܝܬܐ ܕܥܠ ܡܕܝܢܬܐ ܫܡܘܢܝ ܘܥܠ ܐܘܦܝܡܝܐ
ܒܪܬܐ ܕܠܗ̇. ܗ̈ܢܝܢ ܕܡܢ ܐܘܪܗܝ ܡܕܝܢܬܐ ⁘ ܒܝܘܡܝܐ
ܕܗܘ ܠܗ ܕܡܢ ܢܒܝܐ ܪܘܡܝܐ ܕܫܡܗ ܐܢܛܝܪ. ܕܡܪܟܒ ܗܘ
ܡܪܢܐ ܠܬܚܘܬ ܠܒܝ. ܘܠܬܚܒܝܒܝ ܪܘܡܝܐ ܦܪܘ. ܘܬܘܒ
ܡܪܟܒ ܗܘ ܡܪܢܐ ܠܐܠܗܐ ܕܡܪܝܡ ܠܗ ܒܡܫܬܘܬܐ. ܘܟܢܫ
ܢܣܒܐ ܠܬ̈ܫܠܘܬܗ. ܫܠܝܚܐ ܕܝܢ ܐܠܗܐ ܦܘܠܘܣ ܡ̈ܠܐ ܠܝ
ܕܒ ܐܡܪ̈. ܕܢܦܩܘܢ ܠܟܠ ܒܬܪ ܟܠ ܐܠܗܝ. ܕܠܗ ܩܠܝܠ
ܠܗ ܠܟܠܟܘܢ ⁘ ܬܫܡܫܬܐ ܗܝܠ ܕܐܣܛܪܛ ܒܡܕܝܢܬܐ
ܡܒܪܟܬܐ ܐܘܪܗܝ، ܡܢ ܝܘܡܐ ܕܐ̈ܝܠܝܢ ܡ̈ܕܝܢܢ ܡܕܚܝܢ
ܡܡܝܬܘܢ. ܥ̈ܕܬܐ ܕܝܠܗ ܡܬܝܕܥܢ ܘܡܛܝܒܢ ܕܒܕܐܬܐ
2 ܡܕܢܚܬܐ. ܠܒܪܢܫܐ ܚܕ ܡܬܝܕܥܐ ܘܫܪܝܪܐ ܘܛܒܐ
ܠܕܘܟܪܢܐ ܛܒܐ: ܒܠܚܘܕ ܕܝܢ ܡܫܝܚܐ ܗܘܐ: ܡܢ

Variants of the Paris MS (B. N. Syr. 234) = P.

Title in P: ܬܘܒ ܬܫܥܝܬܐ ܕܐܘܦܝܡܝܐ ܘܫܡܘܢܐ ܒܪܬܗ: ܘܬܕܡܘܪܬܐ ܕܐܣܬܥܪܬ ܠܣܗܕܐ ܡܢ ܡܘܕܝܢܐ ܫܡܘܢܐ ܘܓܘܪܝܐ (+ *in mg.* ܘܚܒܝܒ) ܠܣܗ̈ܕܐ ܕܡܢ ܐܘܪܗܝ

3 P ܕܐܘܢܝ 5 P ܕܡܪܟܒ 6 ܦܘܠܘܣ] P <
8 ܠܗ] P < P ܡܟܝܠ 9 ܡܒܪܟܬܐ] P ܕ
ܡܕܚܝܢ] P ܡܬܚܝܢ 10 ܥ̈ܕܬܐ ܕܝܠܗ P < ܘܡܛܝܒܢ]
P ܒܛܝܒܘ 11 ܘܫܪܝܪܐ] P < 12 ܒܠܚܘܕ ܕܝܢ] P <
ܗܘܐ] P <

ܐܬܘܬܐ

L = Cod. Nitriensis nunc Londoniensis, B.M. Add. 14649, *saec.* IX.

P = Cod. Parisiensis, B.N. Fonds syriaque 234, *saec.* XIII.

Unless otherwise stated, the text printed is that of L. All variations of P are recorded in the footnotes.

𝔊 signifies select readings from the Greek versions printed by v. Dobschütz.

ܬܫܥܝܬܐ ܕܐܘܦܡܝܐ

www.ingramcontent.com/pod-product-compliance
Lightning Source LLC
Chambersburg PA
CBHW022016300426
44117CB00005B/219

* 9 7 8 1 5 9 3 3 3 8 7 6 3 *